Adam Smith
and the Founding of
Market Economics

Adam Smith

Eli Ginzberg

With a new introduction
by the author

Adam Smith
and the Founding of
Market Economics

Transaction Publishers
New Brunswick (U.S.A.) and London (U.K.)

The frontispiece is reproduced by permission of Macmillan and Co., Ltd., from *A Catalogue of the Library of Adam Smith*, 2nd edition, prepared for the Royal Economic Society by James Bonar.

New material this edition copyright © 2002 by Transaction Publishers, New Brunswick, New Jersey. Originally published in 1934 by Columbia University Press.

Library of Congress Catalog Number: 2002072673
ISBN: 0-7658-0949-4
Printed in the United States of America

Library of Congress Cataloging-in-Publication Data

Ginzberg, Eli, 1911-
    Adam Smith and the founding of market economics / Eli Ginzberg ; with a new introduction by the author.
        p. cm.
    Includes bibliographical references and index.
    Previously published: The house of Adam Smith. New York : Columbia University Press, 1934.
    ISBN 0-7658-0949-4 (pbk. : alk. paper)
      1. Smith, Adam, 1723-1790. 2. Capitalism. 3. Free enterprise. I. Title.

HB103.S6 G56   2002
330.15'3—dc21   2002072673

TO

My Father

ON THE OCCASION OF HIS
SIXTIETH BIRTHDAY

Contents

Introduction to the Transaction Edition:
The Wealth of Nations *and the Founding
of Market Economics*

The Columbia University Press published my doctoral dissertation, entitled *The House of Adam Smith*, in the spring of 1934. The decision of Transaction Publishers to reprint, in 2002, my long out-of-print dissertation led me to reread *The Wealth Of Nations* for the first time in the intervening seven decades, which reminded me of an earlier speculation.

Suppose that the development of economics had been limited to the publication of *The Wealth of Nations*, and that the new discipline had never heard of David Ricardo, John Stuart Mill, Alfred Marshall, John Maynard Keynes, and many other economists. One could make a case—even a strong case—that economics might have evolved into a stronger and more productive discipline if it had been forced to look to *The Wealth of Nations* for its further guidance. I will do my best to explain to the readers of this early twenty-first century piece why I believe that Adam Smith's *The Wealth of Nations*, published initially in 1776 and subsequently revised by him, warrants such in-depth study.

The uniqueness of Adam Smith's contribution can be summarized as follows: the central question that he raised in *An Inquiry into the Nature and Causes of the Wealth of Nations*—the multi-dimensions of economic growth (and decline) that he dealt with, from the rise and dismemberment of ancient Greece and Rome to the outbreak of the War of Independence between the American colonies and Great Britain—revealed the sophistication of Smith, who emphasized early in his work (chapter 2) "the difference between the most dissimilar characters, between a philosopher and a common street porter, for example, seems to arise not so much from nature as from habit, custom and education. For the first six to eight years of their existence they were perhaps very much alike and neither their parents nor playfellows could perceive any reasonable difference, but the disposition to trade, barter, and exchange alone gave occasion to any (later) difference of talents."

Smith goes on to note that labor is the only universal as well as the only accurate measure of value by which we can compare the values of different commodities at all times at all places.

My recent rereading of *An Inquiry into the Nature and Causes of the Wealth of Nations*, the full title of Adam Smith's classic, called my attention to a great number of important and special characteristics of this masterpiece that had escaped me or that I had not adequately appreciated at the time I wrote my dissertation. Smith set himself a number of basic questions, such as the reasons why some countries, for example Holland and Great Britain, were relatively affluent while many others, such as Spain and most of Italy, lagged far behind. Moreover, despite the recent outbreak of hostilities between the American colonies and Great Britain, Smith offered not a little but a lot of evidence that the working population in the major American colonies had achieved a standard of living considerably in excess of similar workmen in London and in other large cities in the British Isles. Oversimplified, Smith's interpretation was twofold: the first was the surplus of no-cost land for every American farmer who was able and willing to work it; and the second was the continuing willingness of the British government to pay for many of the costs of the colonial government without requiring the local citizenry to contribute much or anything towards these costs.

Little attention has been paid by successive generations of economists to the observation with which Smith brought *The Wealth of Nations* to a close. "If any of the provinces of the British Empire cannot be made to contribute to the support of the whole Empire it is surely time that Great Britain should free herself from the expense of defending those provinces in times of war and of supporting any part of their civil or military establishments in time of peace and endeavoring to accommodate her future views and designs to the real mediocrity of her circumstances."

In seeking to understand the great attraction that *The Wealth of Nations* had for me when I first became acquainted with it earlier in the twentieth century and my even greater appreciation for it from my close rereading of it after the passage of seventy years can best be explained by the following: my amazement at the scale and scope of the challenges that Adam Smith had set himself, not only to understand the dynamics of the British economy in the eighteenth century, but to broaden the scale and scope of his inquiry to include the major stages in the evolution of the European economies current, medieval, and ancient, with further attention to the settlements and later developments of the European migrants to the Americas, South and North, and with at least passing attention to the economies of China and India.

Equally noteworthy is that Smith immersed himself in the historical records of the national developments over multiple centuries that he sought to examine and from which he sought—based on the facts that his probings and analyses would uncover—to extract the lessons from which he could erect his models of growth and development. He was an empiricist, first and foremost. But in addition to being an empiricist, he had held the appointment of Professor of Moral Philosophy at the University of Glasgow, and never avoided the challenge that every serious academic must confront: to choose between right and wrong, better or worse. The principal reason that Smith undertook to prepare a new edition of *The Wealth of Nations* in the early 1780s was to expand very substantially his analyses of the "mercantile system" in which he emphasized the many reprehensible practices of master manufacturers and merchants who engaged in all sorts of disreputable and illegal activities to enhance their earnings by taking unfair and illegal advantages of their customers and their workers. True, many master manufacturers and merchants were responsible for expanding the scale and scope of the market by improvements in their buying and selling of goods and services, but it would be a serious error in Smith's view for the larger society not to seek to protect itself from their nefarious and often illegal actions. While the spread of competitive markets held the best prospects for the improvement in the living standards of the citizenry at large, the courts and the legislature had the responsibility to monitor what was happening in the marketplace so that the mercantile sector could not exploit the consumer.

Two additional observations about my seven decades-infatuation with Adam Smith and *The Wealth of Nations*: I visited Kirkcaldy in August 1939, about two weeks before the outbreak of World War II, in the expectation of learning a little more about Smith's years while he was busy writing *The Wealth of Nations* between the early 1760s and the early 1770s. In seeking the help of the local librarian, he explained that while he had almost nothing of importance relating to the life and work of Adam Smith, he had an impressive collection of testimonials about a young native poetess. Such is fame!

Adam Smith was a firm believer in the role of education in raising the future well being of the population by increasing their knowledge and skills. He strongly favored public financing of village schools such as was the growing practice in Scotland in the eighteenth century. With the advantage of a much lengthened retrospective, I am reasonably certain that my subsequent concentration on the study of human resources during my long academic career was the outgrowth of my early infatuation with the work of Adam Smith and *The Wealth of Nations*, a contribution for which I will always be in his debt.

ELI GINZBERG
2002

Preface

This book is the result of several coincidences. My interest in Adam Smith was first aroused during my senior year in college. One of my fellow students had occasion during a discussion of the *Wealth of Nations* to ridicule the suggestion of Smith that judges should be paid by the litigants rather than by the state. My acquaintance with the history of economics was exceedingly meager but nevertheless the student's criticism did not ring true. He had accused Adam Smith of naïveté. I, however, had never met a naïve Scotsman. A careful reading of the text convinced me that Smith had not been given a fair trial and, after a perusal of the secondary literature, I became suspicious that his general approach had never been fully appreciated.

At about this time, in the winter of 1930, Columbia University acquired the Seligman Library of Economics, a unique collection of economic tracts. I thought it not unlikely that many of the books and pamphlets in this library would shed considerable light upon the background of Adam Smith. Therefore, under the kindly guidance of Professor Seligman, I worked my way through the relevant material which was published between 1688, the year of the Glorious Revolution, and 1776, the year in which the *Wealth of Nations* appeared.

At the beginning of my investigations in the pamphlet literature of the seventeenth and eighteenth centuries, I had the good fortune to make the acquaintance of Professor V. G. Simkhovitch who was then engaged in writing his *Approaches to History*. One who has read these essays will recognize my indebtedness to this scholar.

I have taken certain liberties in the writing of this book which I believe deserve a word of explanation. In Part One the attempt has been made to reconstruct and interpret the *Wealth of Nations* without constant recourse to direct quotation. Adam Smith presents himself; hence, the possibility of unwarranted deductions is reduced. The pamphlet literature of the eighteenth century has been drawn upon to establish a degree of continuity. The dilution of Adam Smith's distinctive style has been intentionally avoided.

In the final preparation of the manuscript, I have been greatly aided by the corrections and additions which the several members of the Faculty of Political Science of Columbia University were kind enough to suggest. I owe a special debt of gratitude to Professors Carter Goodrich and Wesley Clair Mitchell.

NEW YORK   ELI GINZBERG
DECEMBER, 1933

Introduction

Introduction

The South Sea Bubble has just burst; the French Revolution is still far distant. Adam Smith is born during one of the few quiet years of a very disturbed century—a century of wars and revolutions.

He passes a quiet childhood on the north shore of the Firth of Forth, and in his early teens moves to Glasgow to attend the University. He proves himself able and industrious and wins a scholarship for Oxford where he passes six years busily engaged in educating himself, for his professors are interested in things other than their subjects and their pupils.

The middle of the century finds him lecturing to a public class at Edinburgh University on English literature and political economy. Some kind friends have obtained this insignificant post for him. Shortly thereafter, his old University at Glasgow, suddenly remembering his existence, offers him a Professorship in Logic, which he gratefully accepts. The chair in Moral Philosophy, one of the most important and lucrative positions in the University, becomes vacant during the first semester of Smith's academic career. By a stroke of good fortune, the young Professor of Logic is elected to this post.

For thirteen years Smith lectures and writes in this small river town. He publishes a book on ethics that catches the public's fancy, and is a great success. The author's fame spreads far and wide, and pupils come from distant Switzerland to study with him.[1]

At about this time an English statesman weds a wealthy widow and obtains through his marriage not only a wife and money, but also a stepson. As this youth is coming to the end of his teens, his future education becomes a pressing problem. The universities are quite unsatisfactory, and even if they were much better, could offer little to one of the future rulers of Great Britain.[2] Greek and Latin are of slight value to a young duke when he engages in parliamentary debate.

The Continent beckons. Louis XV presides over a cultured, if slightly decadent, court. Voltaire has established himself in Geneva, preaching strange things to the followers of Calvin and Zwingli. The English have long considered French culture to be culture par excellence. Why not expose the young duke to it? If the inoculation takes, so much is gained; if not, nothing is lost. The young man cannot travel alone, for the custom of the day prescribes tutors.

Charles Townshend, the stepfather, passes for the cleverest man in England. In searching for an eligible tutor, he remembers the author of the *Theory of Moral Sentiments*, for the book made a great impression upon him. His son will have one of the most distinguished scholars of the day for his nurse. This statesman is fearless. He precipitates the American Revolution by introducing the hateful taxes and excises which so enrage the colonists. With similar self-assurance, he makes an offer to the renowned Glasgow professor to become his stepson's tutor. Adam Smith accepts, to the amazement of his friend, David Hume, who doubted that he would forego his teaching career.[3] This sceptic momentarily forgot the power of money.

Student and guide sail for the Continent, for France. Paris is slighted at first for a less interesting town in the south, Toulouse, which is the favorite haven of expatriated Englishmen. Here they spend some eighteen months, the former professor becoming increasingly bored as their stay lengthens. The society is horribly dull, and his French is woefully inadequate. His working habits return, and he commences to write a book to while away the time.[4]

Geneva and Paris are visited before the trip is completed. After two and a half years the voluntary exiles return to their native land, the duke somewhat better informed of the world and its people, Adam Smith the richer for his contacts with the Continental intelligentsia, and a life pension of three hundred pounds per annum.

Although he passes some time in London, he spends the greater part of the next decade at his birthplace, Kirkcaldy. The book which he began to sketch in Toulouse is now his chief concern. He is completely preoccupied with its composition, working long and hard.[5] His solicitude for his mother alone prevents him from suffering the ill effects of a too intensive concern with his brain child. His many friends anxiously anticipate the publication of the book, but they are forced to wait a long while. The author will not be hurried. Finally, in 1776, a book appears in London, entitled *An Inquiry into the Nature and Causes of the Wealth of Nations*, by Adam Smith, F. R. S., formerly Professor of Moral Philosophy at the University of Glasgow. Though not so popular as his first book, it is nevertheless successful.

The author returns to Kirkcaldy where he spends the next two years. He receives an appointment as inspector of customs, and is forced to remove his domicile to Edinburgh. Twelve years thereafter, a dutiful servant of His Majesty, George III, passes from this world. His death is almost unnoticed.

In 1926 the leading universities in the world held a sesquicentennial celebration in honor of the publication of the second, and less popular, of Adam Smith's books. Contemporary opinion much preferred the *Theory of Moral Sentiments* to the *Wealth of Nations*.[6] The economic treatise failed to impress the leaders of society. In fact Smith once facetiously remarked that he had almost forgotten he had written the book. The twentieth century thinks it, however, worthy of a jubilee festival.

Systems of thought lead a life independent of their creators and their original environment. Plato died, Greece declined, but *The Republic* lived on. Not really *The Republic*, but legions of *Republics*. Each reader in each generation interpreted the material in the light of his own preconceptions.[7]

During the Middle Ages, the Church was the most powerful institution in Europe. The pontiffs, however, did not find it difficult to utilize the anarchistic doctrines of the Gospels in their struggle for political autocracy. Soviet Russia has followed from the day of its birth a policy of ruthless opportunism but this has not prevented it from persecuting people for being unorthodox Marxists. The present leaders are not bothered by the fact that Karl Marx never wrote one word about the socialized commonwealth.[8] They possess the power of interpretation and anyone who fails to accept their reading of the text is punished.

The Catholic Church did not need the New Testament to authorize the collection of taxes, nor would Stalin be at a loss to construct a Five Year Plan without *Das Kapital*. But as we are all more or less ancestor worshipers or, as Freud would say, sufferers from a father complex, there is practical value in controlling the authorities.

The battle of life is fought with all types of weapons. Ideas are light artillery. As some few of the belligerents might possibly be impressed with intellectual arguments, a cautious tactician will prevent his opponents from adding even such poor ammunition to their war supplies. The good Lord was probably disconcerted by the last European massacre, but that did not prevent both the Germans and the Allies from drafting Him. Each party thought it expedient to have God on its side, if for no other reason than to deny that He was in the camp of the enemy.[9]

Adam Smith wrote *The Wealth of Nations* for many reasons, among them to record his disgust with the chicanery which the merchants and manufacturers practiced. A university, endowed by a merchant prince of the twentieth century, published a volume in Smith's honor.[10] The man who animadverted upon the captains of industry of his time is hailed by the outstanding entrepreneur of a later period. Circumstances can make strange bedfellows feel completely at ease.

English and Continental civilizations were vastly upset during the declining years of Smith's life, and more especially in the decades after his death. The introduction of power machinery caused the disturbance. The problems of the new industrial era demanded attention, and men suddenly evidenced a great interest in economics. Some people became very wealthy; others lost every farthing. The fortunate members of the community were interested in preserving their gains; the victims searched for succor. Political philosophies suddenly developed a high economic value. The successful bourgeoisie were certain that the wise men of the past foretold their conquests when they prophesied that England would be blessed with a great capitalistic economy.

Smith had been a great master of words, and the literati of the new society, in composing their hymns of praise, borrowed liberally from him. At the close of the century his fame was known only to a few discriminating people. However, a short time thereafter, the unfledged writers established him as the father of modern political economy, a national genius of the first rank. Though none had been his pupils, they called him master, searching confirmation for their own theories in his work. It was an artful game of words, and possibly the novices did not realize that it was nothing but a gambol.

Smith has been greatly honored during the last century and a half, but he has also been subjected to vitriolic attacks and violent abuse. He has been praised by his enemies, and condemned by his friends. A series of historical accidents can account for this paradox. During the mêlée the spirit of Adam Smith was lost, but perhaps it is not too late to recapture it.

Part One

Merchants and Knaves

Business is a necessary evil, which the moral leaders of mankind have tolerated but never condoned. At no time did they view with favor the pursuit of material gain. The Old Testament prophets proclaimed against the rapacity of the rich. Jesus scorned the money lenders. Luther had no kind words to say to the wealthy, nor did Calvin indulge the new bourgeoisie.

The eighteenth century was not given to religious exuberance; philosophers and scientists were more prominent in intellectual circles than members of the clergy. The most enlightened people considered God the Great Watchmaker, and his ministers unimportant apprentices. But not everyone was emancipated. The Scottish professor who lectured on economics at Glasgow during the fifties and sixties was not free from the nagging of fanatical Presbyterians. And though he disliked their hard and strict rules of life, he absorbed not a little of their moral fervor. The waning interest in religion resulted in a more intensive study of ethical and moral problems.

The *Wealth of Nations* is a gentlemanly and scholarly, though pointed, indictment of a large group in the society of the day. In common with the reformers of old, Adam Smith looked askance at the knavery and meanness of business men. His wrath was kindled against the merchants and manufacturers, for he hated their invidious practices. He hoped that after the public had been enlightened, remedial action would be taken.

The corruption of individuals is a problem for the courts. The moral degeneracy of an important sector of the population ought to be the concern of the commonwealth. Adam Smith preached to the nation.

The violence and injustice of the rulers of mankind is an ancient evil which scarce admits a remedy.[1] All for ourselves, nothing for others, has long been the vile maxim of masters.[2] The English had decapitated one sovereign and banished another. With the passage of time, they acquired great skill in dealing with the Lord's anointed. They were able to put the fear of Satan into all self-righteous administrators. However, the peoples of other lands were still oppressed by their princes.

England, though fortunate not to have suffered from the violence of the crown, was no earthly paradise. Throughout the greater part of the eighteenth century the country experienced growing pains, but the doctors were unable to diagnose the ailment. Adam Smith, however, was firmly convinced that he had discovered the cause of the malady. The rapacity and monopolizing spirit of the merchants and manufacturers was racking the commonweal's constitution. This was an optimistic conclusion, for he felt certain that the infection was curable.[3] As a careful internist, he paid special attention to the case history.

Since the days of Queen Elizabeth, the legislature had taken trade and commerce under its protecting wing.[4] Delicate plants had to be nurtured with care. It is surprising that the aristocratic landowners who sat at Westminster concerned themselves with the life and fortunes of the urban upstarts, for country folk have never been fond of their city relatives. The action of the noble lords and honorable squires was born in fear and perpetuated in ignorance.

The trading and manufacturing groups played their cards shrewdly, their daily pursuits having schooled them in the arts of deception. They had no difficulty in outwitting and outmaneuvering the untrained and naïve gentlemen, thereby erecting the sneaking arts of underling tradesmen into political maxims for the conduct of a great empire.[5]

Commercial and manufacturing activities on a small local scale were easily comprehensible, but only the expert could fathom the intricacies of international trade. Tillers of the soil could be expected to understand only the most simple business enterprises. In forming opinions on more involved subjects, they were forced to consult the authorities, who were only too glad to furnish them with the necessary information and advice.

A bill became law when a majority in the House of Commons and the House of Lords voted in its favor. The legislators, however, were not truly free agents. They were tools in the hands of a small but vociferous clique. And although bribery was used from time to time, the dutiful members were not properly recompensed for their labors. They were overwhelmed by the craftiness of the mercantile strategists. The ignorance and indolence of the legislators made them docile victims. But even if they had defended themselves, the onslaughts of the aggressors would have been difficult to withstand.

The pleadings of the commercial interests were neither modest nor logical. They followed an extreme opportunistic policy, employing one line of approach until another seemed more suitable. The pliability of their methods was matched only by the rigidity of their objective.

At one period it appeared advantageous to keep the available gold and silver within the country, for mercantile and manufacturing activities could not be conducted without the aid of precious metals. To ship currency abroad would have had unfavorable repercussions upon the internal business structure. Stringent prohibitions were therefore established by the several governments to insure that none of the domestic specie should leave the country. Very severe penalties were established for the violation of this statute.

Economic conditions changed, and shortly thereafter the state adopted a new attitude toward precious metals. The merchants no longer benefited from the restrictions upon the movements of gold and silver. Business profits would probably rise if one could engage in the free import and export of bullion. The old doctrine that the amount of specie reflected the wealth of a country was abandoned, and in its place was substituted the theory of a favorable balance of trade. This shift in economic ideology had certain practical implications. Learned analyses were written for the benefit of the members of Parliament. The business men engaged in polemics with the hope of forcing the government to pass specific legislation which they desired. Many of their petitions were granted, and only the occasional criticism of other groups prevented the legislature from becoming the completely docile servant of the merchants and manufacturers.

Governmental aid to commerce and industry was not entirely above suspicion because it frequently reacted unfavorably upon other branches of the national economy. At recurring intervals, the laboring class proclaimed that the indulgences extended to the trading and manufacturing interests were working to its disadvantage. The shrewd commercial groups quickly established a strong defense, pointing out that unless native mercantile and manufacturing establishments were specifically encouraged, many would give up the ghost. If the privileges were rescinded the working class would suffer most grievously; factories would cease operating and there would be neither work nor wages for the poor. The logic of this argument silenced most of the outbursts.

During the eighteenth century the vast majority of the English people worked the land; the farm element predominated in the national culture. This group was not well versed in political controversy, but occasionally complaints would arise in its midst against the machinations of the business classes. The latter defended themselves most spiritedly, just as they had done in combating the assaults of the laboring poor. In fact, they counter-attacked. They emphasized the fact that the welfare of the farming groups depended upon markets where their products could be sold at remunerative prices. The market was a creation of mercantile genius. However, the traders, being liberally inclined, did not object to the landed interests benefiting from their handiwork. Manufactured goods were exchanged for the surplus products of the land. Merchants who engaged in foreign trade purchased the wares of distant countries with the surplus products of English agriculture, and thereby enhanced the standard of living of the entire nation. The farmers profited greatly by the enterprise of the industrial and commercial classes; hence their complaints were unjustifiable.

The civil servants and the members of the court did not completely trust the business interests, for they feared that certain favors which the mercantile classes received were perhaps detrimental to the welfare of the country. The rights of monopoly made possible the oppression of the many by the few.[6] A wise sovereign knows, however, that his dominions will be prosperous and secure only if the many and not the few are contented. But once again the dialectic talent of the accused did not fail them. They reminded the king that money was the sinews of war.[7] And who but merchants and manufacturers could increase the gold and silver of a nation? If the people were engaged solely in agriculture, no wars could be waged, no victories gained, no territories conquered. In a large measure, the glory and security of the empire depended upon the navy; hence the encouragement of shipping, was one of the most worthy means of employing governmental funds. The grandeur of England was rooted in the prosperity of her manufacturing and the trading classes.

The arguments of the mercantile group might have convinced the laboring poor, the landed interests, and the crown, but Adam Smith who was not artisan, tiller of the land, nor courtier, scoffed at their defense. He bemoaned the success of the merchants' sophistry in befuddling Parliament. Smith hoped that if the public could be enlightened, national policy would become more intelligent. The ignorance of a jury can often account for its obtuseness.

The manufacturers and merchants employed mean and malignant expedients in attempting to further their arrogant demands. They requested a prohibition upon the export of unmanufactured goods, and likewise desired to prevent the import of most foreign wares. They did not hesitate to demand subsidies for native industries, nor rebates upon taxes which they were forced to pay. Their theory proclaimed that no expenditure of energy or money could be too great, if the fortunes of the mercantile classes were involved. The public finally acquiesced in the justice of this doctrine.

During the seventeenth century the death penalty was prescribed for the exportation of unmanufactured wool.[8] English wool was considered to be the best in the world; hence if foreign countries could purchase it, the monopoly of English manufacturers would be broken. Foreign nations were economic competitors and political enemies. It was treasonable to afford them an opportunity of manufacturing goods with English wool. However, if the processing were completed on the Isles, it was not improper for a merchant to sell woolen goods abroad. He could demand a monopoly

price for his wares and hence the wealth of Great
Britain would be enhanced. And although few, if any,
individuals ever paid the extreme penalty for engaging
in the illicit export of unprocessed wool, Parliament
continued to exert itself on behalf of the woolen manufacturers. During the 1740's the woolen trade appeared
to be declining at an alarming rate.[9] Interested parties
probably exaggerated conditions. Some went so far as
to prophesy that England would soon become a prov-
ince of France if more stringent steps were not taken
to prevent the latter country from obtaining a large
supply of British wool.[10] The most elaborate schemes
were proposed to Parliament. No plan of relief, no
matter how fantastic, appeared ridiculous to the merchants and manufacturers of woolen goods, who were
meeting with severe competition in foreign markets.
The government was sufficiently frightened by the
ominous forebodings of the appellants to accede to
many of their requests.

Native manufacturers most frequently demanded
high tariffs, and occasionally they would attempt to
prohibit entirely the import of foreign commodities.
At the time of Adam Smith's birth, duties were levied
on no fewer than twelve hundred items.[11] Most of
these remained in force throughout the century for,
shortly before his death, he remarked that the public
was really unaware of the large numbers of commodities which could not be imported at all, or only upon
the payment of very high duties.[12]

Merchants and manufacturers could combine with
ease, which was of great advantage to them in forcing
their demands through the Houses of Parliament.

They resembled an overgrown standing army which was a constant threat to the government. Naturally, the merchants and the manufacturers received the greatest benefit from the monopoly of the home market.[13] But there was no plausible reason why they should possess a monopoly, for clearly they were more interested in fattening their own purses than in enhancing the welfare of the commonwealth.

Governmental aid to industry, which took the form of restraining the import and export of goods, was of indirect benefit to the merchants and manufacturers. One could not calculate in shillings and pence the advantage which the woolen industry derived from interdicting the export of raw wool. But the business interests were not satisfied with these favors. They demanded direct monetary aid. The powerful linen manufacturers wheedled from Parliament a subsidy upon the export of their goods.[14] They likewise desired to secure their raw products as cheaply as possible. A petition was submitted begging Parliament to remove all duties upon their imports. The legislators agreed; moreover, they established a bounty upon the import of flax.

At the beginning of the eighteenth century, bounties were also granted upon the import of naval stores from America.[15] England used much wood and her forests were no longer sufficient for her needs. The shipbuilding industry was a large customer for tar, pitch, and turpentine. Parliament did not hesitate to make large grants from the public treasury to these trades. Ship construction was profitable without governmental support, but the builders pointed out that they were working for the nation's welfare by increasing the navy. Hence their noble efforts ought to be liberally rewarded. And they were.

To receive governmental favors, it was not essential to engage in a trade which directly increased the security and greatness of England. Bounties were granted on the importation of colonial indigo, as well as on hemp and undressed flax. To bring raw silk, pipe, hogshead, and barrel staves into the country was also considered worthy of public recognition. During the American Revolution, the bounty on American hemp was of little value to British manufacturers. They successfully petitioned Parliament, however, to grant a bounty upon the same goods when imported from Ireland. Not even a war could interfere with the avidity of these patriots.

Drawbacks were of lesser significance, although they again illustrated the ability of the mercantile classes to take good care of themselves. Shipping was an important part of England's economic system. The merchants who engaged in the international transport of goods were greatly hampered by duties and excises. London was the emporium of the world's trade. Silks and satins from the East would often be shipped to the port on the Thames before they eventually found their way to the West. The local restrictions upon commerce greatly handicapped the middleman activities of English shippers. Parliament consented to free the interested parties from many onerous taxes if they presented proof that the goods imported were again exported. Doubtless there existed good reasons for this concession; but the government acted because it dared not balk the demands of the mercantile and manufacturing groups.

The public was apparently convinced by the appeal of the merchants and manufacturers. Adam Smith was not. A tailor does not make his own shoes but buys them from the cobbler.[16] It is equally unreasonable for England to manufacture all types of goods. Every country by virtue of its climate, skilled labor, and natural resources, is especially adapted to produce certain commodities. If all nations would manufacture those wares for which they are best fitted the world would become much richer. What is prudence in the conduct of a private family can scarce be folly in that of a great kingdom.

In the early days of civilization the individual household manufactured all the articles which it needed. Each family was forced to secure its own food, build its own dwellings, and clothe itself. Frequently there did exist some differentiation in the work performed by the sexes. But the history of western civilization illustrates that as cultures developed, men's economic activities became more specialized. The advantages which the world has derived from the division of labor have been inestimable.

The restraints upon trade, instituted at the behest of the mercantile classes, have been detrimental to the welfare of the nation. They have impeded the process of specialization, and have therefore prevented the country from deriving the benefits of a more intensive division of labor.

Industry is limited by capital. Special regulations in favor of specific branches of the national economy

result in a redistribution but not in an enhancement of
the country's capital. There is no reason to assume
that governmental control of investment funds is
beneficial.[17] The individual entrepreneur is highly
rational in the disposition of his wealth, since he
engages in business for the express purpose of making
as much money as possible. A man's exertion in his
own behalf will be more strenuous if he be permitted
to rely upon his own judgment rather than be forced to
execute the commands of a superior authority.[18] It is
preposterous for a statesman to imagine that he can be
as well informed about mercantile and manufacturing
conditions the country over as those actively engaged
in these pursuits.

The merchants and manufacturers constantly impose upon Parliament.[19] To correct this condition the
legislature must cease meddling with industry and
trade. Industrial and commercial activities have
doubtless added much to the wealth and happiness of
mankind, and one must respect the contributions
of the mercantile class to human welfare.[20] However,
the unholy alliance between business and government
which the shrewd traders have been able to establish
need not be tolerated.

The only alternative to a controlled economy is an
uncontrolled one. If the conscious direction of the
nation's economic life has not proved very successful
it might be well to experiment with a free and individualistic system. There is reason to assume that things
might improve if governmental interference were
deliberately abandoned. The granting of a monopoly
to domestic producers was either useless or distinctly

harmful to the country at large. England should have imported goods which foreign manufacturers could produce more cheaply. The desire of the legislature to benefit the merchants and manufacturers forced the country to act otherwise.

Exceptional circumstances can occasionally justify protection to native industries, and in such cases the economic costs of tariffs are not reckoned. Enterprises which are important for national defense ought to be encouraged. Wars are common occurrences; unpreparedness would be foolhardy. Our neighbors are our potential enemies; security must be our primary concern.[21]

The ideal is always confined by the practical. The removal of duties upon imports might be an economic desideratum, but the costs of progress must be carefully checked. In the past, many cumbersome tariffs have been established, but the methods of lowering and removing them must be carefully considered, for untoward disturbances in public life should always be avoided. The practical statesman will proceed with due deliberation because the sudden removal of protection will greatly upset certain industries.[22] Freedom of trade should be established only by slow gradations.

The fear was commonly expressed that the nation would succumb unless Parliament showed the utmost consideration for the welfare of the merchants.[23] The legislators, though for the most part not of the mercantile class, were nevertheless careful to see that the commercial interests should be properly protected. The members of Parliament considered it a matter of honor to care for a group which was unable to plead

its own case at the bar of the House. However, the
invidious propaganda of the trading classes was
largely responsible for this solicitude. The country accepted the theories of the traders as worthy guides
for national legislation. "All degrees of men, from the
throne to the plough, are in mutual dependence upon
the merchant."[24] The nation was held spellbound by
this doctrine. Even the foremost sceptic of the age was
duly impressed with the importance of merchants,
whom he called the most useful race of men in the
whole society.[25] Many favors which had been granted
the commercial classes were justified on the ground
that the activities of the traders were most profitable
to the community.[26] At times the manufacturers and
merchants feared that they had not pressed their
claims with sufficient vehemence. Possibly, had they
been more vociferous, the government would have
been still more obliging.[27] Whenever the legislature
contemplated rescinding some special privilege which
the trading groups enjoyed—a very rare occurrence
indeed—the merchants immediately attempted to
frighten the proponents of the measure. They drew the
most somber picture of the unfortunate chain of events
which would follow upon any unfavorable alteration
of their status.[28]

The solicitude and concern which the government evidenced for the mercantile class did not meet
with Adam Smith's approval. He considered the parliamentary measures which had been passed to enhance
the fortunes of merchants and manufacturers dictated
by private interests and the spirit of monopoly.[29] He
did not deny that the House of Commons probably

acted in good faith, but that did not alter the facts. Fair trade between England and France had almost ceased to exist. The prejudices and animosities of particular traders had been responsible for the various restraints which throttled commerce. Few French goods were able to enter England without first paying a duty of 75 percent. In many cases this impost was prohibitive.[30]

It was frequently contended that the prosperity of a country depended upon its foreign trade. The mercantile system could foresee an increase in national well-being only through the procurement of a favorable balance of trade. But the very advocates of mercantilism did not practice what they preached. It is not surprising that Smith heads his chapter "Of the extraordinary Restraints upon the Importation of Goods" with the phrase, "Of the unreasonableness of those Restraints even upon the Principles of the Commercial System."[31] The program of the merchants was illogical. They promised to enrich England through the sale of goods abroad at the same time that they limited the import of foreign commodities. It was no longer believed that an accumulation of gold and silver could add materially to the welfare of the country. Adam Smith, therefore, failed to comprehend, even upon the principles of the mercantile system, how limitations upon foreign trade could be viewed with favor.[32] One must sell to buy, and buy to sell. The merchants failed to show that it was possible for England to continue selling without buying.

Neighboring peoples were constantly under suspicion. The merchants feared them, especially if they

were opulent. Smith, however, believed that wealthy
neighbors were a great boon to a nation, for prosperous customers were preferable to impecunious ones.
However, the interested sophistry of merchants and
manufacturers confounded the practical sense of mankind. But those who taught these doctrines were not
so foolish as those who believed them. Merchants, at
home and abroad, have preached with passionate
confidence of interested falsehood the dangers of an
unfavorable balance of trade.[33]

Many manufacturers had obtained monopolies
against their own countrymen. The commonwealth
had been steadily bled by the rise in prices which had
resulted from the interference of the government with
the economic system.[34] The merchants and manufacturers had pulled the wool over the eyes of a naïve
public by constantly proclaiming their interest in the
welfare of the state and the glory of the crown. Their
noble words were spoken to hide ignoble acts. Yet it
is perfectly clear that the contrivers of the mercantile
system were merchants and manufacturers whose
major, in fact sole, interest lay in furthering their own
welfare.[35]

Ireland suffered grievously from interference with
her economic life. She manufactured glass but was not
permitted to export it to any country. Raw silk, a
foreign commodity, was under the same restraint. She
was permitted to ship her wool only to England.[36] All
these unjust and oppressive restrictions were the result of the government's desire to cater to the very
slender interest of British manufacturers. England
had absurdly granted a monopoly against herself to

gratify the impertinence of her manufacturers, her merchants, and her workmen. Her loss had however not been solely financial. The machinations of these unscrupulous groups did not end with their raising of prices. These groups imposed upon Parliament to restrict and restrain the freedom of many individuals, assuming that such legislation would benefit themselves. Parliament, the boasted defender of English liberties, forgot her sacred trust and duty and acceded to many of these demands.

An eighteenth-century liberal could not view with favor the circumscriptions upon the rights of citizens. The English government was the most advanced of all the governments of Europe. It was the pride of cultured men both at home and abroad. Adam Smith, after a careful study, concluded that the success of the mercantile system was illusory. The economic restrictions upon the members of the commonwealth were surely to be condemned. But the merchants had succeeded in corrupting not only the economic but also the political institutions of the land.

Commerce had not always hampered the freedom of individuals. The development of trade and industry in the fourteenth century was largely responsible for the disintegration of the medieval system which had been founded upon restriction and restraint. Liberty and security, order and good government, were in no small measure due to the liberalizing influences of the new economy which rose upon the ruins of the medieval state. The merchants and artificers of that period acted in the light of their own self-interest, but proved themselves to be the unconscious directors of a great revolution.[37] The encouragement which English liberty received from these classes ceased in part when they succeeded to power. Ever since the reign of Elizabeth, Parliament had been obeisant to the commercial interests. Occasionally the legislation desired by the merchants helped to democratize political institutions, but in most cases the granting of their petitions had the opposite result. The class which had done so much to free both individuals and property from medieval restrictions was constructing a new society where liberty would once again be unknown. No merchant would admit that he was endangering the freedom and liberties of Englishmen. The power of the word is great, and liberty had become hallowed and sacred. No one dared mock at the shibboleth. The mercantile interests were more concerned with profits than with slogans; but the avidity of the merchants came into conflict with the prevailing ideology.

The merchants and the manufacturers, in pursuing their objectives, were constantly forced to go against the grain of the political philosophy of the day. The pamphlet literature of the eighteenth century confirms this dissonance. The commercial and industrial interests were constantly advancing projects which ignored the liberties of English citizens. The best that could be said is that they were indifferent to the struggles of English emancipation. Their concern with their own affairs made them lose their sense of humor completely. A merchant who desired to set up a complicated scheme to prevent the export of raw wool, remarked that free subjects must not be burdened with restraints.[38] Another keen critic of contemporary economic life reached the conclusion that trade needeth only liberty and protection.[39] If, perchance, some contradiction existed between these two approaches, either one could be sacrificed. A writer who favored the widespread establishment of bounties upon exports, did not fail, in the introductory passages of his work, to state that liberty, encouragement, and protection were the great conducive means toward the augmentation of the people.[40] He believed that the economic system of England derived great advantages from freedom of sale. At the same time he felt certain that many benefits could be obtained from the more widespread introduction of monopolies.

Encouragements to industry entailed, in most cases, restrictions upon the freedom of individuals. Writers might advocate the adoption of the most illiberal schemes, but they were forced to pay lip service to *liberty* in order to avoid being accused of anti-English prejudices. It was even believed that all things have a natural propensity to liberty.[41]

Most people agreed that trade and liberty mutually reinforced each other.[42] Trade could never flourish without liberty. Analysts frequently pointed out that the prosperity of the Low Countries resulted largely from the liberal nature of their governments. But though they were greatly impressed with the advantages which trade derived from liberty, they did not hesitate to advocate many measures which restricted freedom. They favored the strict regulation of Irish trade; they favored the most elaborate tariffs.[43] A writer who ascribed the prosperity of the country to the liberal nature of its constitution did not hesitate to lobby for the most restrictive registry system.[44]

One appealed to liberty not only to procure new favors, but also to secure old ones. Parliament at one time contemplated restraining the use of gold and silver lace. The manufacturer of this material feared that his industry would be ruined. He submitted the following brief: In a recent edict, that autocratic sovereign, the Czarina, stated that she would be distinguished from her subjects even though fifty thousand of them were undone. Such action in a backward country could be appreciated. But for a liberal state to impoverish many people because the populace was indulging in luxuries was incomprehensible.[45] One writer was shrewd enough to realize that restraints were truly serious only in those countries where the people had liberties to lose.[46] A poet became lyric in singing the praises of freedom which, in his opinion, was the soul of commerce, the source of a nation's wealth and happiness, and the most sturdy support of the state.[47]

The confusion was tremendous. The babble of special pleadings became most disconcerting to the quiet student. But a few sceptics were able to see the forest for the trees.[48] The people were bewitched by the word liberty. All crimes could be committed under its ægis. All is fair in love, in war, and in a struggle for liberty.

Adam Smith was a resident of Glasgow when John Watt, the instrument maker, attempted to settle there and pursue his trade. The town did not have an instrument maker in its midst, but Watt was refused permission to establish himself.[49] The jealous tradesmen probably sang hymns to liberty every evening of the week, but no class intended to hurt its own interests by practicing what it preached. Smith made a very careful study of the methods which the various groups employed to further their own ends. They prattled about the liberal aspects of the mercantile system, but he realized that one must attend to the nature of the thing and not pay any regard to the word.[50] He ridiculed their practices because he held freedom in such high regard.

At the beginning of the eighteenth century a clever essayist remarked that honesty was the best policy, but that trade offered more and more opportunity for knavery.[51] The author of the *Wealth of Nations* accumulated during the course of his researches ample evidence to support this contention. And he drew the logical conclusion from this unorthodox premise. Merchants and knaves must be prevented from continuing to corrupt the economic and social life of the people.

Farmers and Gentlemen

The heart of a nation's culture throbs most violently in its urban centers where the inhabitants are
most frequently in a state of flux. The people of importance live within the city confines. Revolutionary
movements customarily originate in populated regions.
The vitality and excitement of cosmopolitan existence
contrast violently with the drabness and stability of
country life. One of the severest critics of modern
civilization, Karl Marx, was so depressed by life on
the land that he considered farmers not much better
than barbarians.[1]

Adam Smith was born during the second decade of
the eighteenth century in a community which engaged not only in tilling the soil, but also in fishing
and smuggling. His birthplace, Kirkcaldy, though
but forty miles from Edinburgh, was much behind the
times, for the natives still used nails for currency.[2] The
residential capital of Edinburgh with its dirty streets
and narrow houses was likewise not very impressive.[3]
Glasgow, one of the most important cities in the
country, where Smith both studied and taught, was
just commencing to expand.[4] In his student days the
town could not boast of a single bank, and by the
middle of the century, it had but twenty thousand
inhabitants. Many people admired urban civilization
despite its shortcomings, but Smith could not grow

enthusiastic. He was not in the least disdainful of the vast majority of his fellow citizens who lived upon the land as their fathers and grandfathers had done, totally indifferent to the antics of their urban cousins.

Karl Marx was not the first to deprecate the innate qualities of the plowman. Adam Smith related that in his time the farmer was generally regarded as the pattern of stupidity and ignorance. However, he dissociated himself from this popular prejudice, for he did not consider the agriculturalist deficient in judgment or discretion. No other vocation requires such a variety of knowledge and experience. The yeoman, not accustomed to social intercourse, might appear strange and awkward when compared to the city laborer. But this is of slight importance for, when superficials are disregarded, it becoms clear that the people of the country are superior to those of the city.[5] The husbandman must be skilled in many pursuits, while the city laborer need know but one trade.[6]

At the dawn of history, the sons of Adam were tillers of the soil. Only after Cain had been guilty of the heinous crime of fratricide, was he forbidden to engage in agriculture. The cultivation of the soil was the original destiny of man and he will always retain an inherited predilection for this employment.[7] But even if man were not by nature favorably predisposed to agriculture many would become tillers of the soil because of the attractiveness of country life.

The citizenry of an agricultural nation is in the greatest degree kind and good-natured. Whenever merchants and manufacturers form a large part of the

population, a country is likely to be selfish and adverse to all social intercourse.[8] Smith lived among
the farmers of Kirkcaldy, and among the merchants
of Glasgow. Possibly his own experience led him to
dogmatize about the superiority of an agricultural
to an industrial community.

The entire nation evidenced great concern for trade
and industry, but was generally indifferent to the
landed interest. However, the Select Society of Edinburgh, of which Smith was a member, often debated
means and measures for improving agriculture.[9] This
club was composed of the leading intellectuals of the
residential capital. In 1756 a resolution was presented,
calling for the admission of a group of farmers in order
to make the discussions on agriculture more realistic.
One of the distinguished founders of the club thought
it beneath the dignity of the society to admit these
men, and furthermore criticized severely the utilitarian trend of the program. Adam Smith was of a
different opinion. He took an active part in furthering
these unorthodox practices.[10]

Smith's interest in, and sympathy for, the land and
its workers did not impair his critical faculties. He disliked monopolies, and he well realized that the ownership of land was a monopoly. In very early times, land
had been common property, and it became divided
only after civilization reached a high stage of development. But when the earth's surface had been
staked out, the landlords, like all other men who
love to reap where they have never sown, demanded
a rent for the natural produce of the soil.[11] At one time
the laborer had been able to gather the fruits of the

earth and retain them for himself; now he was forced
to share his harvest with the owner of the land. Rent,
or the price paid for the use of land, is a monopoly
price. It is determined not by the expenditures which
the lessor has made, but by the maximum payments
which the lessee can afford.[12]

The foe of monopoly and special privilege had developed a very strong case against the landowners.
He did not fail to disclose in great detail their
peculiarly intrenched position. But he did not de-
duce from his analysis that private property in land
was wrong. Smith was liberal, not radical. He accepted
the property relations of British society of his day.
There is no contradiction between his abhorrence of
monopolistic restraints and his failure to attack the
ownership of land, the greatest of all monopolies. He
was not willing to unsettle the major buttress of the
existing system. Private property must be tolerated,
but many reforms could be undertaken to insure its
more equal distribution. Until the coming of the
Messiah this world will never be completely rid of
sin, hence the economic system will contain depraved
elements. Man had best concern himself with expiation.

Some men own land while others work it. This
arrangement cannot be basically disturbed without
disrupting the entire economic and social system. But
it would be distinctly possible, in fact very much
worth while, to reform this imperfect institution.
During Smith's lifetime about one-fourth of all the
land of Scotland was under entail.[13] An owner could
establish regulations concerning the division and sale

of his land which would bind his heirs centuries after
his demise. This custom had arisen in feudal times
when there existed strong prejudices against the
alienation and dismemberment of large estates. But it
was ridiculous for the common law to respect this
ancient usage, which was based upon the absurd
supposition that every successive generation did not
have an equal right to the earth and its produce. The
fancies and theories of a man have no right to burden
his descendants hundreds of years after his departure
from this earth.

Likewise, the right of primogeniture had been
turned from a transitory into a permanent evil. During
the decline of the Roman Empire, the leaders of the
northern tribes engrossed large portions of unculti-
vated lands. This action was not beneficial to the
public welfare, but the major damage might have
been avoided had the institutions of entail and primogeniture not been established. The laws of inheritance
alone prevented the large estates from being parti-
tioned.[14] The barons had usurped advantages through
the establishment of these legal norms, for they advanced an exclusive claim to the great offices and
honors of the country. But they could never have
established their title had their financial position not
been unimpeachable. A poor nobleman is a pitiful
specimen. Therefore in order to enrich the head of the
house all the children were beggared. The institutions
of entail and primogeniture were likely, because of the
prevalence of family pride, to endure for many years.

The wealth of a nation depended in no small
measure upon agriculture, hence all forces which in-

fluenced the fecundity of the land were most important. There was no reason to subscribe to the extreme
view of the Physiocrats, who held that agricultural
labor alone was productive. The ingenious and learned
speculations of the Continental economists were
amusing but hardly worthy of detailed examination,
for they were clearly both false and harmless.[15]
Nevertheless, it was true that farm laborers were
more productive than artificers, merchants, and
manufacturers.[16]

Agriculture ought to receive every possible encouragement because it contributes more than either
industry or trade to the wealth of a nation. Institutions like entails and primogeniture, which hamper
the productivity of the land, should be immediately
reformed.

The lord of a manor seldom applied himself to the
improvement of his estate because he preferred to
spend his time and money in more interesting ways.
One could derive much more enjoyment from ostenta-
tious and luxurious living than from the onerous
tasks of scientific farming. Occasionally a wealthy
squire would exert himself in an effort to run his
estate efficiently, but in most cases his lack of knowledge and perseverance would nullify his good intentions.[17] The improvement of the land presupposes
the use of a careful system of accounting in which
small losses are balanced against small gains. Furthermore, expert supervision is necessary. The great pro-
prietor has not been schooled for such work.[18]

The liberalizing of the English constitution had
been a great boon to the yeomanry; it contributed more

to the present grandeur of Great Britain than all the
boasted regulations of commerce.[19] But despite the
advantages which liberty and security had afforded,
agricultural progress had been slow. Much arable
land could not be leased because wealthy proprietors
used it for preserves; and the farmer paid very high
rent for the land which he did cultivate. Furthermore, the improvements which he made redounded to
the advantage of the owner. He made therefore most
reluctant to exert himself because the larger part of his
efforts enhanced not his own but the landlord's fortune.
For these reasons little new capital was invested in
land. The independent merchant would not withdraw
his funds from business and transfer them to agriculture. In commerce he was not forced to share his
profits; in agriculture he had to divide his gains with
the landowner.[20]

The state had done little to further the specific
interests of the landed class. The established system of
private property was advantageous to the landowners,
but this was a most general benefit which merchants
and manufacturers also shared. Perhaps a review of
the relations of the landed group to the commonwealth could aid in promoting the welfare of both.

The landowners had made periodic attempts to
cater to their own interest by passing what they assumed was beneficial legislation. The country gentry
had frequently obliged the merchants and manufacturers by legislating in favor of commerce and industry. Finally, they caught the habit and bestirred
themselves in their own behalf.[21] It must be recorded,
however, that they were much less given to the

spirit of monopoly than the commercial classes, for combinations among them were well-nigh impossible.[22] They were also much less aggressive than the merchants. No jealousy need exist among landowners, for one man's crop could never influence market prices. Improvements in agriculture are never patented because the enhancement of a neighbor's production does not spell one's own ruin. The commercial aspects of farming differ entirely from the pecuniary phases of all other business enterprises. Therefore, it is not surprising that the squires' attempt to promote their own interest through parliamentary legislation was not very successful.[23] They lacked the shrewd training which the merchants and manufacturers received in their daily pursuits.

The enactments which the legislature had passed in favor of agriculture were of little or no value. The landed gentry placed their greatest faith in grain regulation. They established a bounty upon the export, and levied duties upon the import of wheat. In addition, the shipment of live cattle from Ireland was interdicted for many years.[24] But the protectors of English agriculture looked upon the bounty as their most potent weapon. It raised the price of native corn and facilitated the conquest of foreign markets; but it was doubtful whether the agricultural subsidy could withstand careful scrutiny. The majority of the benefits were probably illusory. True, the bounty raised the price of corn. It must be remembered, however, that the price of corn determines the price of all other commodities, and to increase its price would result in increasing the price of all other goods. The general cost of living would rise, but this would not be advantageous to any group. More corn would find its way abroad, and less would be consumed at home, but the large export would have a deleterious effect upon the industrial welfare of the country. A rise in food prices would force wages up, with the result that the cost of production of English manufacturers would increase. The bounty, by cheapening the export price of corn, aided foreign manufacturers. It enabled them to keep wages low, and hence reduce their operating costs. Their products, therefore, could compete more successfully with English wares. Parliament was handicapping English commerce and manufacturing without rendering any substantial service to the landed interest.[25]

The bounty was not only to be deprecated on economic grounds; upon occasions it led to the most unfortunate upheavals in the social system. Dearths were wont to occur from time to time, and occasionally they would develop into famines. The bounty on corn increased the misery of a lean year. Parliament frequently suspended the bounty upon exports and the duties upon imports when a great scarcity arose. But the damage had already been done. The subsidy upon the export of corn during the years of plenty had prevented the accumulation of surplus stocks.[26] England prospered during the eighteenth century, and the bounty frequently received the credit for the improved condition of agriculture. The relative security and freedom which English citizens enjoyed were doubtless more responsible for the progress than the bounty and twenty other absurd regulations of commerce.[27]

Defoe had remarked at the beginning of the century that a state of civil war existed between the landed and the commercial classes.[28] He, as well as most pamphleteers after him, deplored this struggle. Few people took the trouble to write and to publish tracts for scientific reasons. One did not petition Parliament in order to enlighten its members upon obscure issues in economic theory. Practical considerations motivated the authors of most books and pamphlets on political economy. The trading and the manufacturing classes were the most frequent appellants. It is not surprising that one often reads in their economic brochures of the inseparability of interest between the land and commerce. The suspicions of the farming faction had been aroused on several occasions by the measures which the mercantile group had attempted to force through the legislature. The scepticism of the landowners forced the merchants and manufacturers to advance this thesis of the harmony of interests. The public expected to be misled by men who consulted their own interests, and the traders therefore had to feign a deep concern for the landed class in order to secure their own ends.[29]

Manufacturers who desired to prevent the export of unfinished woolen goods had no difficulty in proving that the landowners should be as interested as themselves, if not more so, in the establishment of this embargo.[30] The landowners were begged to consider how greatly the value of their estates would rise if the woolen manufacturers flourished.[31] This appeal to the landed gentry was especially strong in the forties when the country was swamped by proposals to raise the price of wool. It was pointed out that "by what means soever trade is improved or decayed, by the same means the value of land will infallibly rise or fall."[32]

All true lovers of Great Britain were concerned with the creation of a favorable balance of trade.[33] The wealth of the country depended upon an excess of exports over imports, and the manufacturing and the commercial interests could alone secure this favorable balance. England could not export large quantities of grain. With the steady increase in her population, the differential between her production and her consumption was constantly diminishing. The gentry, therefore, were forced to admit that the prosperity of the country depended to the greatest extent upon the industrial and the commercial classes. If traders grew rich, landowners would likewise be affluent, for it is trade alone which raises the value of land and its products.[34]

The closest affinity should exist between the objectives of the mercantile and the agricultural interests. If England were to trade only with herself or her colonies, she could never grow rich, for her wealth depended entirely upon commerce with other nations.[35] The welfare of the landlords will always be closely correlated with the vicissitudes of external trade.[36]

Occasionally a writer would deny the axiom that the bond between trade and agriculture was mutually advantageous. He would doubt that the encouragements to trade benefited the landed interest. Among these skeptics was a learned and liberal clergyman whose knowledge of commerce exceeded his ac-

quaintance with the geography of heaven and hell.
He inquired whether the landed gentlemen in excluding foreign labor and establishing tariffs were not
acting against their own welfare.[37] Perhaps they had
been duped by the monopolizing tradesmen. The mercantile classes felt called upon to answer these attacks, but they presented a most unsophisticated defense. They reaffirmed their belief in the mutual inter-
dependence of agriculture and trade, emphasizing
their conviction that the decline in one branch of the
economy certainly would foreshadow a depression in
the other.[38]

The merchants were vultures who preyed upon the
ignorance of the country gentry, silencing all discontent by fear and intimidation. They maintained that
only the stupid are suspicious. The proprietors of the
large estates were, of course, not unlettered, but their
schooling had failed to instruct them in matters of
trade and commerce. The public's indifference to
problems of political economy was likewise most dis-
tressing. The author of an invaluable and erudite
work on wool, which Adam Smith quoted on several
occasions, remarked that the good people of England
were scarcely willing to consider this important subject. He stated that some believed conditions could
not be improved. Others assumed that they possessed
an intuitive understanding of trade and commerce,
and hence were able to arrive at valid conclusions
more by trust than by examination. The pessimists
contended that all who were not bred from early
childhood to trade and manufacture would always remain unenlightened despite their diligence and in-

quisitiveness. Finally, the landed interest having embarked upon the same bottom as trade, decided to leave the steering to the merchants and the manufacturers.[39]

When any branch of trade showed signs of declining, there were always public-spirited citizens who exerted themselves on its behalf. The people who suffered from depressed business conditions were certain to offer suggestions and advice to Parliament. In most cases they were able to apply sufficient pressure to instill life into their proposals. When agriculture was in need, one could seldom discover an interested soul, since the country gentlemen never evidenced great concern for their own welfare. The friends of the landowning class presented schemes for raising the value of land only upon the rarest occasions.[40]

It passed generally for gospel truth that the merchants and the manufacturers were the solid foundation of English economic society. However, some few dissenters believed in the doctrine that the country could be prosperous only if the landed interests flourished. If the income of the landowning groups declined, tradesmen suffered because customers would be more niggardly in expending their shillings.[41] Adam Smith sympathized with the minority, for he believed that the country could not be affluent unless agriculture prospered.

The advancement of agriculture should have preceded the improvements in industry and trade, but because the several governments have interfered with their respective economic systems, the reverse movement has taken place.[42] The landed interest could have benefited greatly by forcing the government to cease its meddling. But instead of fighting against the favors which had been extended to the merchants and manufacturers, the landed groups applied for similar consideration. If the corn trade were supported, money would be plentiful, foreigners would invest their funds in England, and rentals would increase. To neglect this traffic would be most dangerous. It is always preferable to cherish a few important trades than to squander ineffectual aid on all.[43] The cost of production of wheat was less in other countries than in England, and therefore a bounty ought to be established, for clearly this staple deserved as much consideration as other commodities.[44] The farmers also demanded bounties on beef, butter, and cheese to compensate them for the favors which Parliament had bestowed upon industry and commerce.

At times the moans and groans of the country gentlemen became very audible. They greatly resented the disabilities under which they labored. A Quaker wrote that "all men are convinced that all taxes, all interest on stock and money, all manner of burdens and encumbrances whatsoever, do either immediately, or ultimately fall upon the land-holders."[45] The respectable members of society did not pay much heed to the statements of a despised sectarian. At the same time they must have secretly sympathized with the complaint of the Quaker.

The stirring of the long-docile country gentlemen somewhat disturbed the commercial interests. The land-owners were forthwith accused of ignorance and stupidity because they looked with an evil eye upon the gains of the trader.[46] They were likewise held responsible for the loss which the country suffered from the large emigration. The landed interests, in their desire to enforce religious uniformity, caused the exodus.[47] Less stupid people would recognize that they were willfully bleeding themselves to death. It was estimated that the gentry lost forty shillings for every person who left the country.[48]

Adam Smith listened to the trading interest but was not greatly impressed with its plea. He was convinced that merchants were not citizens of any country, and was therefore amused by their appeal for public support on the basis of patriotism.[49] The commercial and the industrial groups had worked upon the self-love of men by affecting to trade for the public good.[50] Actually, they had imposed upon the generosity of the country gentlemen. Unfortunately, the landed interest acted very foolishly, for instead of attacking their opponent's strongholds they busied themselves with setting up their own defenses. But it was not too late for the agricultural group to shift its tactics. There existed every likelihood that if the intrenched position of the commercial and the industrial interests could be undermined, agriculture would be greatly benefited. Nothing could be lost by experimenting; much might be gained. So thought Adam Smith.

The Laboring Poor

The Bible recommended the care of the poor; Solon enacted legislation in favor of the oppressed debtors; the Roman senate provided bread and circuses for the urban proletariat. The records of the past, however, do not deal in great detail with the life and the activities of the vast masses of the laboring poor. The wisdom of Solomon, the oratory of Pericles, the conquests of Caesar were considered more worthy of description than the struggles of the common people. The rulers of the state despised the populace, and, except in times of crisis when man power became important, ignored it completely. During normal periods the commonalty had to labor hard, pay high taxes, and behave itself. Art, politics, and learning were the vested interests of the rich and the powerful.

The poverty of the Middle Ages was appalling. All were poor. After the fall of the Roman Empire the gulf which separated the common people from the nobility narrowed greatly. The church state had to be most circumspect in dealing with the laboring poor, for they formed almost the only group in medieval society. After many centuries of want and deprivation the economic horizon commenced to brighten. The disintegration of feudalism, the increases in foreign trade during the period of exploration, and the break-

down of the autocratic power of the Church, did
much to pull Europe out of its long depression. The
satins of the East and the exotic fruits of the West
became well known.[1] A rich class reappeared. The
cleavage between the courtiers and the peasants
broadened. Money once again became the mark of a
man, and he who was poor was ignoble.

From the reign of Elizabeth until the outbreak of
the French Revolution, British statecraft worked hard
to increase the power and wealth of the country. The
programs of national aggrandizement did not fail to
include the working population, although no unanim-
ity of opinion existed as to the proper rôle of this
group. Would increasing their numbers be a boon to
British prosperity? Would limitations upon their
freedom be of value to English manufacturers? These
and similar questions perplexed the rulers of England.
However, at no time was the discussion primarily
concerned with the welfare and happiness of the laboring poor. Peasants and artisans had not been created
by a wise Providence in order that they might live
happily and contentedly. Theirs was a higher destiny.

The eighteenth century revolted against many
ideas and institutions of earlier times. One of the most
startling insurrections in the realm of thought was the
new approach to the study of man. For the first time
in history, philosophers became vitally interested in
the welfare of the populace. The Professor of Moral
Philosophy at Glasgow was pleased by this change;
in fact, he helped to bring it about.

Smith was not the first to advance the theory that
all wealth is derived from labor. A medieval church-

man and a seventeenth-century philosopher had developed a labor theory of value. Smith, however, broke new ground in building a complete system of economic thought around the concept of productive labor. The opening lines of the *Wealth of Nations* illustrate the importance of his approach. He believes that the annual labor of every nation originally supplies it with all the necessaries and conveniences of life.[2] The earlier writers in analyzing the economic order had woefully underestimated the significance of the laboring man. They were too concerned with the activities of the manufacturer, the merchant, and the farmer to pay much attention to the simple artisan. In Smith's treatise the laboring poor occupy a position of primary importance.

The labor expended upon the manufacture of a commodity establishes its value. The quantity and quality of the country's total production is in large measure determined by the ability and dexterity of the working population. All techniques and institutions which affect the skill of the laboring groups are therefore most important because they directly influence the wealth of a nation.[3]

Smith's emphasis upon the hitherto most neglected stratum of society was most radical, and it is not surprising that he ran into difficulties in developing his thesis. In the past, land had always been viewed as a productive force in the national economy; capital had likewise not been considered sterile. Smith's presentation of labor's claim conflicted with the vested rights of land and capital. It soon became clear that some compromise would have to be established, because the

intrenched position of the older claimants was very
strong. Even as attorney for the plaintiff, Smith had
great respect for the defendants. Their prestige rather
overawed him. Although he at first contended that
labor was the sole determinant of value,[4] it was not
long before he admitted that rent and profits might
also influence value.[5] This compromise contained
many implicit contradictions, which Karl Marx almost a century later devoted some time to eradicate.
He succeeded, but only to a limited extent, for though
he strengthened the weak links in Smith's chain of
reasoning, he added new ones which proved none too
strong.[6]

Adam Smith, however, wrote a very interesting
brief, despite its deficiencies in logic. The history of
the world was in his opinion the history of the increasing efficiency of labor.[7] The absence of specialization in antiquity accounts for the poverty of that
period. The agriculturist could improve the yield of
his crops only if he were able to make an intensive
study of the land. He was, however, forced to spend a
considerable part of his time in securing food, shelter,
and clothing for himself and his family, and was
therefore unable to devote his entire energies to the
care of his plants. Some members of the community
showed great talents in the chase, while others proved
to be expert house builders. After many centuries of
development it became clear that the entire group
would benefit if each member engaged in that activity
for which he was best fitted. A hunter could kill
within a very short time more deer than he could
possibly use for his personal needs. A thatcher was

able to put his own dwelling into condition by two weeks' concentrated effort. A farmer, working on fertile land, could raise more than he could consume. The several specialists commenced to exchange their surplus commodities and labor power, and very soon the wealth of the community increased. An economic society could be most efficiently organized upon the basis of specialization and exchange.

The first book of the *Wealth of Nations* is devoted almost entirely to an analysis of those forces which facilitated the division of labor among men. The treatment afforded the working population becomes highly significant in an approach which considers national progress to be largely determined by improvements in the specialization of labor. Merchants had maintained that English prosperity was due to their trading activities. The farming population had contended, although less frequently, that they formed the backbone of the national economy. Adam Smith, however, asserted that the welfare of all countries, at all periods in the world's history, depended upon the status of labor and the development of the industrial arts.

The theorists before Smith had not viewed the workingman as an important element in the national economy. True, traders were forced to employ sales clerks; manufacturers could not get along without factory hands; and wealthy landowners needed men to work their fields. Former generations, however, considered the laborer important only because he aided the merchant, the manufacturer, and the farmer in fulfilling their economic functions. Their attitude toward labor was not only narrow but actually perverse. The older writers, reflecting the opinion of the ruling class, maintained that a state could be powerful and wealthy only if the laboring population were kept under strict control.

During the sixteenth, seventeenth, and eighteenth centuries English laborers were greatly oppressed by the apprenticeship laws which the masters strictly enforced. The parishes, in a vain attempt to keep the poor rates down, added to the tribulations of the workingman by holding him prisoner in the town of his birth. The state did its bit to make the laboring poor completely unhappy by heavily taxing the commodities which they used. It was deemed good policy to deal with the working population in a high-handed fashion. The fortunes of the rich depended upon the penury of the poor.[8] From the days of Queen Elizabeth, Parliament did little to improve the status of the impoverished and docile working population. In the fifth year of the reign of that sovereign the Statute of Apprenticeship was passed. It provided that no one could ply a trade unless he under-went a seven-year period of training. The avowed purpose of this act was to insure the purchaser against shoddy and imperfect goods for clearly no artisan would lack skill after so long a tutelage. The legislators further believed that the statute would form young people to industry.[9]

Corporations with exclusive privileges were established better to enforce the apprenticeship regulations. A society of master artificers obtained from the government an exclusive right to engage in trade or

manufacturing within a specific area. The masters
were frequently permitted to establish rules and regulations for the conduct of their business. In most cases
the charter members of a corporation limited the
number of people who might engage in their trade.
This procedure insured their special privileges.

In the middle of the eighteenth century there were
twelve important corporations in the city of London.
Only a member of one of these companies could be
elected Lord Mayor. In addition, there existed seventy-
nine other corporations each possessed of privileges of
lesser significance.[10] It was customary for a youth,
after obtaining the consent of his parents, to bind
himself for a period of seven years to a master in one of
these ninety-one corporations. If, perchance, his employer were indifferent, the young man might pass his
entire time in drudgery, acquiring no skill whatever in
his craft. Not a few masters drove their apprentices
like slaves, exploiting them to the utmost. Some few
concealed the secrets of their business in order to keep
their pupils in a state of dependence.[11]

Novices, upon the payment of an entrance fee, received free board and lodging in return for fourteen
hours work per day.[12] They were likely to waste their
time and cheat their masters at every turn for they received no wages and therefore had little reason to be
interested in their work. The conscientious hireling
was promised the protection and assistance of Divine
Providence but unfortunately he would not be rewarded until the hereafter.[13] An apprentice, after
seven years of service, became a journeyman. He then
received wages for his labor and secured a modicum of

independence. In theory but not in practice, a journeyman might become a master after several years' additional service. Without wealthy relatives one could
never hope to become the head of a trade for often a
capital of several hundred or even thousand pounds
was required.[14] But money was not always a trust-
worthy sesame; at times even it was unable to unlock
the powerful doors which the old masters had built to
keep out newcomers.

The apprenticeship regulations were undoubtedly a
great boon to the masters, for it enabled them to secure
much free labor, and enchanced the prices of their
commodities by reducing competition. Parliament refused to alter radically the Elizabethan legislation because in its opinion the public was not oppressed by
these measures. It likewise denied that the restrictions
upon the workingman violated the rights of English
citizens. The government viewed with favor the apprenticeship and corporation laws for it believed that
the public benefited from the regularization of industry. However, it really was an impertinent affecta-
tion to maintain that any good could result from
legislative measures which trampled upon the most
sacred property of man—his labor.[15]

People of enlightened views deprecated the restraints upon the workingman not only on political
but also on economic grounds. They scoffed at the
pragmatic defense which the advocates of regulation attempted to establish. The claims of the
mercantilists that the apprenticeship regulation inclined young people to work could not be substantiated. Man would never exert himself were it not for

the rewards which industry promised. Apprentices
who received no wages were therefore lazy and indifferent. The lengthy period of service which the
apprentice was forced to undergo was entirely unjustifiable, because a young man of average intelligence could be taught the tricks of any trade within a
few weeks.[16] Many maintained that corporations
raised the quality of workmanship but this was most
doubtful. The best check upon fraud and negligence
would be to offer the consumer an opportunity to deal
with competing groups. Unfortunately, under existing conditions the monopolistic privileges of the
corporations forced the buyer to purchase his goods
from a specific individual, at a definite price, irrespective of the quality of the merchandise. It was often
necessary to go into the suburbs to have a piece of
work tolerably well executed. Corporations were
urban institutions, but they did possess the right to
exclude competing goods from their territory.[17]
Smuggling was therefore not uncommon.

The Statute of Apprenticeship was probably less
baneful to the working population than were the
other restrictions upon labor. Corporate monopolies
not only raised the rate of profits but also enhanced
the wages of certain laborers.[18] The increase in wages,
however, was not sufficient to compensate for the
disabilities of apprentices, especially for their enforced period of free service. The laboring poor would
gain greatly from the repeal of this statute. A liberal,
despite his general distrust of all repressive measures,
might have tolerated the apprenticeship laws if they
had benefited the wage toilers. One could have dis-

liked bounties and yet not have attacked them, if the poor were directly aided by their enactment. The payment of public monies to those engaged in the herring trade might have been indorsed if the price of fish had thereby been reduced, for the poor could then have purchased their food more cheaply. A noble end might have justified the use of ignoble means.[19] But the act passed in the fifth year of Elizabeth's reign regulating the conditions of labor did not show a net balance after a careful audit. Hence liquidation was in order.

The apprenticeship laws doubtless obstructed the free circulation of labor and were therefore detrimental to the true interests of the working population. The Settlement Acts were even more injurious. During the sixteenth century the relief of the poor was in a most chaotic condition, and toward the end of Elizabeth's reign a law was passed with the aim of establishing some semblance of order in the dispensation of public charity. Local responsibility was established, and henceforth each parish would be forced to care for its own indigent members. Each municipality therefore studied means of preventing the numbers of its poor from increasing. The law provided that a parish did not have to assume responsibility unless the individual could prove that he had resided therein for forty consecutive days. The village overseers were in effect transformed into detectives whose primary duty was to discover potential charges. The justices of the peace could be petitioned to remove a newcomer unless the latter were able to rent a house for ten pounds a year or give security to the amount of thirty pounds. Those citizens of the British Isles who were so shortsighted as to have chosen parents without means became for all practical purposes prisoners for life in the town of their birth. The few who refused to suffer the consequences of their bad judgment were not likely to improve their condition by bold action. They might trek the highways, but their fate was far from enviable. If they succeeded in hiding the place of their birth they would be sent from parish to parish, for each village would desire to relieve itself of responsibility as quickly as possible. The venturous souls were not at all certain that they could remain outside the clutches of the law, for their poverty marked them as potential criminals. At any time they might be haled before a justice of the peace and, if unable to account for their past and their present, be convicted of poverty and sentenced to be transported. The penalties for this serious crime had been modified as the legal code became more humane. In former years, the indigent poor were liable to whipping, ear-piercing, branding, and decapitation with and without benefit of clergy. The enlightened eighteenth century retained corporal punishment, but evidenced its progressiveness by substituting transportation for the more barbaric penalties of old.[20] The judge, if in an indulgent mood, might show the vagrant extreme kindness and not order him to be transported, but press him instead into the army or the navy.[21] Regular gangs abetted the magistrate in the performance of his judicial duties. These ruffians would overwhelm a poor man and hale him into court. If he failed to give a satisfactory account of himself he would be ordered to board a man-of-war or to enlist as a common soldier.[22]

The life of the docile poor was not much happier than that of the vagrants. A child whose parents had either died or disappeared was most unfortunate. The community would hand the youngster over to anyone who would offer room and board, in exchange for his labor. One lad relates that at the age of five he was working ten hours a day for his meat and drink. His master, fearing that he might run away, confined him to the house and the yard before the door. Upon his employer's death this happy existence came to an end. The boy was then forced to shift for himself, eating when he found employment, starving when he had none.[23] The rich did everything in their power to enforce the biblical injunction that he who does not work shall not eat. If the poor, seeking employment and finding none, asked charity, they were whipped as sturdy beggars; if they stole in order to feed themselves and had the misfortune to be caught, they were hanged for thievery.[24]

Most people agreed that a large population was the best criterion of a country's prosperity. The number of England's inhabitants was doubtless increasing during the seventeenth and the eighteenth centuries. There was one serious drawback to the nation's progress: her poor were augmented with every increase in her general population.[25] During the second decade of the eighteenth century one estimate placed the number of unprofitable poor at a million and a half.[26] As only a very small fraction could be transported, the vast majority had to be supported at home by the landed and the commercial interests.[27] The care of the poor developed into England's most important

industry. The burden was especially severe upon the
landowners. The land tax was very high. Parish
officers did everything in their power to ease the situation, even committing murder in the interest of their
economy program. Nor did they hesitate to defy the
king's court in order to save their fellow taxpayers
and themselves some paltry shillings.[28]

During the reign of George I the Settlement Acts
were amended. Several communities felt that the cost
of poor relief could be reduced by rationalizing the
outmoded techniques, and therefore petitioned Parliament to permit the erection of workhouses. The poor
were to be housed in dormitories and forced to work
for their food and lodging. The parish officers hoped
that great economies would result from institutional-
izing the indigent. But the erection of workhouses
required large amounts of capital, and though many
were established the reform was not generally
adopted.[29] The great increase of robberies which took
place during the middle of the century could be explained only by the desperate condition of the poor.
One writer believed that workhouses offered the only
solution and suggested that they be erected with private funds, if state monies were not forthcoming.[30]

After a century and a half of experimentation the
methods of poor relief were still most unsatisfactory.
The liberties of Englishmen had been severely curtailed in an attempt to solve this perplexing problem.
The law ordered people to starve at home though they
might find suitable employment abroad.[31] The various
regulations violated natural liberty and justice without achieving any practical results. Unfortunately the

common man, after suffering from these oppressions
for more than a hundred years, had not yet rebelled.
His docility is all the more remarkable when one
remembers that "there is scarce a poor man in England
of forty years of age . . . who has not in some part of
his life felt himself most cruelly oppressed by this ill-
contrived law of settlements."[32]

The state never hesitated to pass the most drastic
labor legislation. The Settlement and Apprenticeship
Acts interfered with both the supply of laborers and
the conditions of labor. At an early period the government usurped control over the very heart of the labor
contract by legislating on wages. The Black Plague
radically reduced the size of England's working population. Parliament, fearing a rise in wages, outlawed
all private bargaining between employers and employees. Those seeking work were ordered to present
themselves in the market square on an established
date, at which time the officers of the crown would
announce the scale of wages. In most cases a maximum
rate was stipulated and it was illegal to pay or to receive more than this amount.[33]

During the many centuries that the magistrates
fixed the hire of laborers, wages were kept low.[34]
Though in Adam Smith's time the judges no longer
exercised this prerogative, the legislature did establish a maximum rate of wages for workers in the
garment trade. Governmental regulation was however not customary.

The attempt of Parliament to settle disputes between masters and workers usually results in a decision
favorable to the former, for the wealthy and powerful

classes counsel the government. Therefore, whenever a law enhances the welfare of laborers, it is just and equitable.[35] For instance, Parliament in prohibiting employers from paying their workmen in kind rather than in money, acted most honorably, for it prevented unscrupulous masters from exploiting their laborers.[36]

The laws of conspiracy prove, however, that the legislature has not always acted chivalrously. Workmen cannot form combinations to raise wages or to improve working conditions, though employers are not prohibited from operating in concert. The law reinforces the economic disabilities of the weaker class, because master manufacturers can organize so much more easily than their employees. In fact, the former are always in a constant and uniform combination to insure their rights and advantages, and social ostracism is visited upon the employer who acts independently. In case of struggle, the workingmen are always in an inferior position, and therefore use either violence or outrage; they must frighten their masters into an immediate compliance with their demands. A landlord, a master manufacturer, or a merchant can live for a year or two upon his accumulated stocks, but the savings of the laboring poor are not sufficient to prevent them from starving to death within a week.[37] Despite these odds in favor of the wealthy and powerful groups the state throws the weight of its authority against the weaker party. Masters demand and obtain the rigorous execution of the severe anti-combination laws. Were the state to act impartially, it would likewise prosecute masters for conspiracy, but unfortunately government is always class government.[38]

Labor legislation was not the only scourge of the working class. The taxation system was certain to have important, though indirect, repercussions upon its welfare. Mercantilism had perverted the true principles of public finance by employing taxation not only for revenue but also for monopoly.[39] Parliament was unable to levy the most equitable and efficacious taxes because it was constantly preoccupied with the establishment and the furtherance of monopolies. The government utilized all the means at its disposal to aid British merchants and manufacturers, and occasionally the pursuit of this design injured the laborers. However, the hurt which it inflicted was superficial. Without governmental aid, English commerce and manufacturing might languish, with the result that labor could have neither work nor food. The class interest of the parliamentary legislation could not always be disguised behind protestations of concern for the very people who were the subject of attack. The government deliberately attempted to whittle down the standard of living of the laborers, hoping to satisfy the manufacturing group by placing at its disposal a cheap and docile working force.

The cry had often been raised that the laboring population of England was indolent and slothful, and that a worker who earned enough by three days' labor to keep him for a week would spend the rest of his time in riotous dissipation.[40] The payment of low wages would put an end to this nonsense, and force the laborer to be industrious.[41] A project was discussed which contemplated importing a large number of German workmen in order more successfully to reduce the wages of native employees. It was abandoned only after the evidence proved that Germans ate and drank at least as much as the English.[42] Many observers of British culture were shocked by the prevalent use of luxuries, for every poor family drank tea at least once a day, and ate wheaten bread instead of loaves made from rye and barley.[43] The self-appointed defenders of English civilization begged Parliament to stem these decadent tendencies, and the government strained itself to accede to their requests.

Excises were levied on many commodities which the poor consumed: soap, salt, candles, leather, fermented liquors were all subject to tax.[44] To increase the cost of these products would force the working population to lead more simple and frugal existences. There would be no funds for debauchery, no time for licentiousness. Laborers would have to work six days in the week to earn enough to keep themselves alive. One of the keenest critics of English society was certain that the laboring population would never become industrious until the cost of living was raised.[45]

Adam Smith had not the least sympathy with the philosophers of this school. He deprecated the heavy taxation of necessities; future generations would suffer if the poor were unable to give their children a proper upbringing. If the laborers' wages were lowered their offspring would probably suffer from malnutrition and exposure.[46] Taxes which fall on a necessitous person are always cruel and oppressive; the worst taxes are those which bear more heavily on the poor than on the rich.[47] For instance the window levy was most unjust, for the poor could no longer afford to have either light or ventilation in their homes.

The taxation of the poor cannot be supported even by mercantilistic arguments. A careful analysis proves that taxes upon labor or upon commodities used by labor are certain to be paid by their superiors. If the subsistence of wage earners were reduced their efficiency would be impaired and manufacturers would suffer. The latter, in order to protect themselves, would probably raise wages. In either case the middle and upper classes would be forced to bear the burden.[48]

The policy of England was to keep the laboring population servile and industrious. Merchants and manufacturers, fearful that they would have to foot the bill if the laborers improved their condition, attempted to stifle all social reform. No respectable member of English society would have advocated raising the standards of living of the laboring poor. Adam Smith, however, was Scottish and was therefore not oppressed by the taboos which prevailed south of the Midlands. He did not hesitate to emphasize the facts that rent and profits eat up wages, and that the two superior orders of people usually oppress the inferior one.[49] Furthermore, he pointed out that unless circumstances force them, the wealthier classes never act generously or humanely in their dealings with their less fortunate brethren. Manufacturers loudly bemoan the high wages which they pay their workmen, but remain silent when profits are discussed. If the public complains about the dearness of commodities, the shrewd business men lose no time in placing the blame upon the high rewards of labor, forgetting to mention that their own rate of return might possibly influence prices.[50]

During the seventeenth and eighteenth centuries the vast majority of English statesmen exerted themselves to keep wages as low as possible in order to encourage trade and industry. But they were only partially successful. The laboring population were receiving more than a bare minimum, though their wages were seldom so high as their enemies maintained.[51] The leaders of English society bemoaned their inability to prevent the improvement in the condition of the working class. Educated people were depressed by this progress, for clearly it could come to no good end. There was, however, a singular philosopher who believed that the group which fed, clothed, and lodged the whole body of the people, had a right to be tolerably well fed, clothed, and lodged itself.[52] But he was a queer academician. Men of affairs knew that the laborers had no rights, although they ought upon occasion to be pitied and patronized.[53]

It was fantastic to fear high wages, for whatever improves the general welfare of the greater part of the community can never be considered an inconvenience to the whole. Poverty is a great social liability. An able laboring population is possible only if workers receive ample remuneration for their efforts; hence to complain of the liberal rewards to labor is to lament the effect and the cause of the greatest public prosperity. As wealth increases, wages increase, and therefore population increases, all of which is for the good of the commonwealth.[54]

The effect of high wages upon the laborer has never been properly studied. Workingmen are more active, diligent, and expeditious in countries where they receive large rather than small rewards. The contention that high wages make for riotous living is without foundation; men do not work four days a week in order to spend the remaining three days in the pub. It is the strain of their work which forces them to take prolonged and frequent rest. Masters might well listen to the dictates of reason and humanity, and moderate rather than intensify the application of their workmen. Disorders generally prevail in the economy of the rich, but in the homes of the poor, workmen frequently ruin their health by excessive diligence. When piecework is well rewarded, laborers frequently overstrain themselves in their desire to improve their position. Many men have a working life of less than ten active years.[55]

Industry has been carried on for the benefit of the rich and the powerful, to the neglect and oppression of the poor and the indigent.[56] Civil government, so far as it is instituted for the security of property, defends the rich. Adam Smith hoped that the government would eventually exert itself in behalf of the poor,[57] and make it unnecessary in the future for them to pray daily to the

Gracious Lord God, who has opened thy hand and satisfied us with good; who hast clothed the naked, filled the hungry, and gathered the poor who were scattered and solitary into one house; affect our hearts with a deep sense of this thy goodness towards us; And mercifully grant that always being exercised in good works and not cherishing sin with the bread of idleness we may use thy liberality to thy glory, and walk worthy of so great benefits in sobriety of life, in the obedience to our Governors, in brotherly love one towards another, and in constant obedience to thy word. Pour down thy blessings on this whole parish; and grant, we beseech Thee, that as our necessities are daily relieved out of their abundance so their wants may be supplied out of thy riches; for Jesus Christ his sake, our blessed Lord and Savior. Amen.[58]

Big but Bad Business

Rome declined, and Western civilization all but disappeared. For many hundred years after the sacking of the city on the Tiber, the peoples of Europe lived a very barren life, for the cultural achievements of antiquity were lost, and no new ones were created. The economic wealth of Greece and Rome had likewise vanished.

During the Middle Ages man tilled the soil to keep himself from starvation; he spent some time in the manufacture of simple clothing to protect himself against the rigors of the climate, and to conform with the morals of the Church. For the most part he lived in miserable thatched huts, in imminent danger of succumbing to the cold. Under such conditions of life there were no surplus products to exchange; trade and commerce were practically unknown. The established institutions reinforced the death grip which poverty had upon business enterprise.[1] Money was constantly under suspicion, and the ever-watchful Church fathers constantly tormented the soul of the merchant. The state and the law did their best to throttle what little trade there was. Life and fortune would be risked in shipping goods down the Rhine from Frankfort to Cologne. Each petty prince would attempt to extort, rob, and often kill the venturous spirit who sought his fortune a few miles from home.

In view of these circumstances, the economic stagnation of the Middle Ages is no mystery.

During the many years that the Papal See reigned over Europe, life was strictly regimented. The priestly hierarchy was primarily interested in the community and not in the individual. The Church during the years of its ascendency did not tolerate deviations from the *status quo*. But after many centuries the absolute sovereignty of the Bishops of Rome was contested, and successfully undermined. The reforming divines of the north, in their struggle against papal corruption, preached the doctrine of individual rather than communal responsibility for the human soul. This new theology in taking root among the dissenters exercised important influences not only on the religious but also on the economic life of the people. The community lost its authoritative direction of business activities. Henceforth the individual would not be molested if he worked hard, practiced thrift, and avoided luxurious living.[2] The peddler principle of turning a penny whenever a penny was to be got was no longer banned as the gospel of the devil.[3] The medieval Church, convinced of the fallibility of man, trusted no one, and therefore regulated life minutely in the light of her superior understanding. The fifteenth and sixteenth centuries were willing to gamble on the individual, and the tremendous increase in the wealth of nations during this period has often been ascribed to the success of this speculation.[4]

The Protestant countries revised their moral and ethical outlook, and thereby facilitated the economic reforms which were taking place. But Francis Drake, pirate par excellence, was also a product of this period, and it is not unlikely that his prizes contributed as much to the commercial expansion of Great Britain as did the sermons of Archbishop Laud.

The leaders of the medieval Church despised wealth for they could not achieve it. Gold and silver were much rarer than saints and devils. After the discovery of the New World by an Italian in the employ of Spain, money became more plentiful. England gained most from the good fortune which should have been Spain's. She obtained much wealth by force, for the British navy was not only a national ornament but also a most efficacious instrument of economic exploitation. It served the nation and served it well. But a vicarious existence is an uncertain one, and the spoils of combat cannot last forever. The English established an empire in the hope that the new wealth would be secured for many centuries to come. Colonial settlements were the philosopher's stone.

The Protestant countries denied the authority of the Church, but their kings soon usurped the rights and privileges which the ecclesiastical institution had formerly possessed. England immediately before and after the Reformation was much the same country. A reform but not a revolution had taken place. Government and business had been intimately associated during the Middle Ages, but government and business had both been unimportant. A close relation likewise existed between the political and the economic spheres during the commercial revolution. But at this period the setting was less somber: states were powerful, and business lucrative.

Adam Smith considered the discovery of America and the opening of the trade route to the Indies via the Cape of Good Hope the most important events in the history of the world. The new continents greatly increased the economic horizons of Europe.[5] While Spaniards stripped the Indian nations of their valuables,[6] the northern countries adopted a different means of securing the wealth of the New World. The French, Dutch, Swedes, and English colonized the new lands, and were moderately successful in their attempts. The Anglo-Saxons, however, had the good fortune to see their sparse settlements grow until a great colonial empire stretched along the western shores of the Atlantic.

At first the mother countries, discovering that they could secure but little gold and silver from their outlying possessions, lost interest in them. Soon new products made their appearance on both sides of the ocean. The division of labor increased, and important improvements in the industrial arts took place under the stimulus of the new trade. The European monarchs upon learning that tobacco and rum could be turned into gold and silver, quickly took control of the colonial trade. Kings have always needed money and they had no intention of neglecting such an excellent opportunity to fill their coffers. The privilege of exploiting the wealth of the New World was not, however, opened to all. Charters with exclusive rights were sold at profitable prices. The crown and the merchants coöperated in establishing trade monopolies. The sovereign ceded lands which he did not possess to his subjects who wished to develop settle-

ments which did not exist. The merchants and the
manufacturers alone were in a position to exploit the
El Dorados of the New World, and the crown therefore did everything in its power to aid these groups.
The colonial policy of the country was dictated by the
allwise merchants.

Parliament was most anxious to secure for England
the exclusive advantages from colonial trade. The
legislators were constantly perturbed by the prospect
of other countries deriving any benefits from trade
with the English settlements. They therefore, in the
hope of safeguarding British interests, placed very
severe restrictions upon colonial commerce.[7] The
business men engaged in the North American trade
were anxious not to lose any pennies unnecessarily.
Actually, their rate of profits was exorbitant. The interest of both the mother country and the colonies
was sacrificed to these agents. Nevertheless, the crown
continued to indulge them. The prohibitions levied
upon the colonies because of the groundless jealousy of
merchants and manufacturers were a manifest violation of the most sacred rights of these people. The
disorder and injustice in European countries had
originally stimulated the settlement of these foreign
outposts. Had there been no religious and social persecutions the colonies would probably never have been
founded. But unfortunately, the policy of European
countries had been to dampen and to discourage their
victims even in their new retreats.

The colonies prospered despite the restrictive
measures which the mother countries attempted and
in most cases succeeded in establishing. The abundance

of good land which could be had almost for the asking was a great boon to the new settlers; but the liberty to organize their affairs in their own way was largely responsible for their progress. Foreign trade might be laid under restraint but there was little interference with their domestic concerns. The institutions which impeded the growth of the mother countries were not transplanted to the western hemisphere. Entails, primogeniture, corporations, regressive taxes were not found in the colonies. Unexhausted soils and virgin forests were certain to enrich the enterprising immigrant.

The mercantilists assumed that the traders who monopolized colonial commerce greatly enhanced the wealth of the mother country. Adam Smith thought otherwise. The attempt of European countries to establish exclusive trades with their colonial possessions could only prove unprofitable to both parties. To prohibit the colonies from buying and selling as they saw fit was very foolish, for it laid a dead weight upon one of the most certain springs of business activity.[8]

The merchants naturally did not object to the existing arrangements because their monopoly enhanced their profits.[9] The nation however paid dearly for the prosperity of this small group. An excess of capital was employed in the colonial trade; hence, because of the interference of the state profits rose above their natural level. The galling bands of monopoly led to a serious dislocation in the apportionment of the nation's resources and therefore lessened the annual wealth of the country. England, by interdicting

the direct export of tobacco from the colonies to the
Continent, doubtless gained a relative advantage over
her enemy, France. By controlling this trade she could
force her neighbors to pay more dearly for the privilege of smoking, but no country could obtain any
absolute advantage by the mean and malignant project of excluding as many nations as possible from
trade with its colonies. France, if she were forced to
pay an enhanced price for Virginia tobacco, would
increase the price of Canadian furs. The monopoly of
colonial trade is an invidious expedient which hurts
the mother country even more seriously than the
colony. "It is a project altogether unfit for a nation of
shopkeepers; but extremely fit for a nation whose
government is influenced by shopkeepers."

It is not clear why statesmen and economists considered the colonies to be valuable assets, for a review
of the books by competent auditors would doubtless
have proved them to be liabilities. A colonial empire
can be of value to a nation of shopkeepers only if it
strengthens the military or the financial power of the
mother country. The English colonies did neither.
England found it necessary to supply men and money
to defend the colonies against their own enemies, but
the dependencies in no way recompensed the national
exchequer for these outlays. There could be no excuse
for England to waste the blood and gold of her citizens
in behalf of a people which would sooner forget than
remember its heritage.

The merchants had cajoled the nation into this
expensive and foolish policy, and the costs of colonial
administration were really a bounty in their favor.

The country in securing the commercial classes a monopoly and high prices did not act in a niggardly fashion. Six times and more in fifty years it took up arms in the interest of colonial trade.

The commonwealth lost money on its colonies and yet it did not part with them. National pride prevented the adoption of a rational policy. Concerns which run at a loss are liquidated; imperialistic enterprises which do not show a profit should be abandoned. Perhaps it was visionary to suggest the voluntary surrender of the provinces, but if they did not add to the strength of the nation they were worthless appendages to which the knife should have been applied. Good money should not be thrown after bad. If the plan to establish a successful colonial empire proved impracticable, it should have been given up.[10] Expediency, however, must bow to vanity and give way to private interest. The vested classes which benefited so greatly from colonial trade were ardent supporters of the existing system. Any attempt at reform, in view of their opposition, was well-nigh doomed to failure.

England progressed during the centuries in which its colonial empire expanded. Many students naïvely assumed that the home country would never have prospered but for the advantages which it secured from its dependencies.[11] Evidence in support of this contention was, however entirely lacking.

The far-flung English dominions comprised only a small percentage of the total area of the globe, but there was no reason to confine British commerce to these regions. Trade with independent nations under certain conditions could also prove profitable to the inhabitants of Great Britain. The crown however limited the numbers who might engage in foreign trade upon the assumption that a restrictive policy would prove most lucrative.

One of the earliest international trading companies was that of the *Merchant Adventurers* which received a charter from the king in 1505. The members of this corporation traded primarily with western Europe, and only indirectly with more distant peoples. During the fifteenth and sixteenth centuries many new trade routes, especially to the Far East, were discovered, and the sphere of commerce was thereby greatly enlarged. Quickly the several European countries established companies with exclusive privileges in order to monopolize as much of the new trade as possible. It was assumed that unless the rate of profits were high, no capital could be enticed into this traffic. The special indulgences which had been granted the companies at the time of their establishment were long continued.

The exclusive companies had been given a free hand in the administration of their affairs, but they had unfortunately abused their freedom. The East India Company had been especially badly managed, and the inhabitants of the Far East who fell under its control had been grievously oppressed. The overseers often willfully destroyed the goods of the natives in order to enhance prices; in fact their rapaciousness often denuded entire regions.[12] The oppressive and domineering mercantile company could have been held responsible for the backward condition of India.[13]

The English crown, in its desire to facilitate the efforts of the merchants, permitted them to exercise sovereign powers; hence the exclusive company usually became the virtual ruler in the districts where it traded. However, economics were more important than politics. The directors and the stockholders were much more concerned with dividends than with the welfare of the natives. A mercantile company, not unlike a merchant, is forced to make profits quickly and consistently if it desires to remain in business. The transitory gain of a monopolist is of much greater importance to a commercial undertaking than the more permanent revenue of a sovereign. But ignorance, and the meanness of mercantile prejudices, prevented the directors from perceiving that their true interest coincided with the interests of the country which they ruled.[14]

The directors at home were as inefficient as the agents abroad. They were negligent and profuse in the disbursement of other people's monies. The proprietors were neither informed nor interested in the affairs of the company, beyond the point of receiving dividends. Hence the directors could rest assured that if the company were indifferently managed they would not be held to account.[15] If the exclusive companies were stripped of their privileges, they would succumb to the competition of private traders. Even under existing arrangements, the large corporations were hard pressed by the merchants who dealt on their own account, though the latter were subject to heavy taxes. An owner would always evidence more care and vigilance in the supervision of his business than a

salaried manager. The monopoly of foreign trade
sacrificed the interests of the nation to those of the
merchants. Certain trading corporations, however,
were dying a slow death, and the public need no longer
fear them. Others were unfortunately still very much
alive and did give one cause for concern.

In the middle of the eighteenth century, the Hamburg Company, which at one time had controlled
most of England's export and import trade with
northern Europe, was practically defunct.[16] It had
once been very oppressive, but the interlopers succeeded in breaking the monopoly. The company
deserved praise for having become completely useless.

The Turkey Company, which controlled the trade
to the Near East, had been most exclusive. No one but
a freeman of London was eligible for admission and
then only upon the payment of a high entrance fee.
Goods to the Levant had to be shipped through the
port of London. This was a most onerous regulation,
for land transport from one part of England to another
exceeded the direct water freight charges to the Near
East. The success or failure of the corporation's investment depended upon the ability of the foreign factors.
The company maintained for business reasons an
ambassador and several consuls in Turkey. The
government should take over the diplomatic corps
and at the same time open the trade. Monopolies were
solely interested in increasing their profits by raising
prices, and the public's sole protection lay in the
establishment of competitive conditions.

The African Company attempted to regulate
English trade with the Dark Continent. For many

years it transported Negroes to America, but the
enterprise had not proved profitable. The Dutch, the
Portuguese, and the French were very serious rivals.
The English Company believed that by establishing
fortifications along the coast, it could gain the upper
hand over its competitors. Parliament was receptive
to this plan and extended considerable credits;
furthermore a heavy tax was levied upon private
traders. The servants of the company dealt in gold
dust, elephants' teeth, dyeing drugs, and the like,
but with no great success; the failure of these highly
speculative undertakings finally led to the decline of
the corporation.

The South Sea Company became famous more for
its vices than for its virtues. Early in the eighteenth
century it obtained a monopoly in supplying Negroes
to the Spanish West Indies, but this privilege under
the mismanagement of the directors turned into a
liability. The company possessed a large capital, and
was unable to discover sufficient opportunities to invest it in trade. It turned therefore to banking,
submitting to the government a plan whereby it
would assume the responsibility for the entire national debt in return for a widespread monopoly of
England's foreign commerce. Parliament accepted the
proposal, and shortly thereafter in 1720 a tremendous
speculation in the company's stocks took place.
Within six months an 800 percent rise occurred. Then
the bubble burst. Adam Smith used restrained language when he referred to the knavery and extravagance as well as the profusion and negligence which
prevailed in the management of the company.

The English government was in fiscal difficulties at the beginning of the eighteenth century and the East India Company came to its rescue with a very liberal loan. This corporation had encountered hard sledding ever since the Revolution of 1688, undergoing several reorganizations within a few years. Its ability to oblige the government saved it for some time from further difficulties, for Parliament renewed its charter. But as the century advanced, attempts were again made to revoke the monopolistic privileges of the East India Company on the ground that England did not obtain the maximum benefit from this trade.[17] The service which the company had rendered the exchequer on several occasions was at first sufficient to secure it against these new attacks.[18] However, the pressure upon Parliament to free the trade to the Indies, increased and probably could not have been withstood had it not been for the emergence of a new issue. By the middle of the century the trade rivalry between France and England resulted in a large-scale war for the ultimate political control of India. The East India Company bore the brunt of the struggle and after many a hard campaign emerged as victor. The British government was naturally inclined to indulge the corporation after its successful conquest, but the small band of merchants found it increasingly difficult to rule a nation much larger than England. Parliament though it permitted the company to retain many special rights and privileges, was forced to assume control. Further mismanagement by private interests left the government no alternative but to enlarge its direction over Indian affairs. It was not until the second decade of the nineteenth century that the trade to India was finally opened.

The regulated and joint-stock companies were not very successful in the conduct of their business; their employees were largely to blame.[19] Resident many thousands of miles from home, they had little fear of the directors. In most cases they were more interested in their own speculations than in the speculations of their employers. Many were proved to be dishonest, although the larger proportion did not engage in direct fraudulent practices. The servants of a trading company were prohibited from engaging in private trade but this regulation was more observed in breach than in practice. Even the chaplains managed to turn a penny here and there during the hours when they were not ministering to the souls of men. The officials of a large company did not fail to harass and ruin all those who attempted to interfere with their personal business pursuits. The natives suffered more from the invidious practices of the petty official than from the far-flung activities of an exclusive company.

Adam Smith was opposed to monopolies. He was, however, willing to admit that when a hazardous trade was first undertaken, some justification might exist for the establishment of a company with special privileges. Although he disliked business organizations to usurp sovereign powers, he countenanced the erection of military fortifications in order to safeguard their trading activities. The sword often helped to make the pound secure. But Smith denied that monopolies need be continued for more than a few score years. Companies which possessed exclusive privileges over a long period have almost invariably mismanaged their businesses. The unlimited permission of companies to erect fortifications has also led to unfortunate consequences. Shortsighted merchants have frequently declared war, capriciously and cruelly.[20] Monopolies should have short lives because their economic and political activities are almost always injurious to the commonwealth.

The crown however, remained indulgent of the joint stock companies. The alliance between government and big business continued to exist, though the public suffered therefrom. The reason is not far to seek. States have always been in need of revenue, and England during the seventeenth and eighteenth centuries formed no exception to the rule. The South Sea and the East India Companies were, until they ran into difficulties, both very good friends of the exchequer. The state did not let them down until it became clear that their resurrection was no longer a possibility.

Certain government officials were extremely solicitous of the companies' welfare. These bribe-takers were very clever machinators; Parliament was putty in their hands.[21] The public remained docile for it felt that the government could efficiently supervise the business activities of the large corporations.[22]

The trade to the Indies, Turkey, Africa and the South Seas was probably quite considerable. During the middle of the eighteenth century the East India

Company showed profits of about half a million pounds annually.[23] It seems doubtful, however, whether the prosperity of Great Britain depended upon trading companies. Big business, despite its occasional success, had proved to be bad business. Adam Smith had no tears to shed over its failure. Private vices could never result in public benefits.

The Costs of Evil

There never has been and probably never will be a truly democratic society. Differences in power between members of the same community are the *sine qua non* of gregarious living. There can be no general without an army, but there can be different types of armies.

In ancient Egypt a slave upon the demise of his master was occasionally put to death; in the society of that day a menial servant had no independent status. In Rome, a domestic who had displeased his lord was ordered to be cut into pieces and fed to the fish. During the Middle Ages, a small group of noblemen placed the most severe limitations upon the persons and property of the vast majority of the population.

At the beginning of the eighteenth century, the condition of the poor, especially in England, had changed somewhat for the better. The lower strata of society which had been for the most part severely oppressed in former centuries now possessed a substantial degree of freedom, though one would have had no difficulty in perceiving that a journeyman tailor and a Yorkshire squire did not belong to the same class. The laboring poor and the wealthy gentry were not equals. But the country gentleman could no longer force his tenants to remain upon his land as had been his privilege in bygone ages. In certain regions the tillers of the soil still performed obligatory services for the land-lord but they had otherwise shaken off all vestiges of feudal servitude.[1]

The law had become increasingly democratic, but a more powerful force embittered the life of the poor. Money succeeded in impeding the progress which should have resulted from the liberalizing of the English government, for

It can not do everything but still it can do a great many things. It will blind the eyes and make black appear to be white. It will shut up the bowels of compassion and make a man naturally good-natured do the cruellest things for the sake of obtaining it. It will gradually wear out all sense of shame and bring its votaries to do the most infamous things without blushing.[2]

Adam Smith well appreciated the potency of money, for he recognized that in the society of his day economic power was perhaps more important than political domination. He did not ignore the fact, however, that votes in Parliament could easily be transformed into gold in the pockets of the merchants.

The world could be greatly improved by removing many inequalities which prevented men from realizing their full potentialities. Smith did not desire to level all differences between the several classes. He restrained his reforming spirit. It would be preposterous to deprive the wealthy of their riches in order to secure only the worthless equality of universal poverty; but it would be both expedient and just to reduce the fortunes of certain individuals if the well-being of the majority could thereby be enhanced.[3] Smith's attention was directed especially toward those institutions which enabled a small minority to enrich themselves at the expense of the large majority.

The Scottish economist was primarily concerned
with increasing the wealth of nations, and therefore
analyzed in detail those forces which facilitated or
impeded the realization of his aim. At first glance the
activities of farmers, laborers, and merchants appeared
to be all for the best. The land produced food sufficient
to feed not only the tillers of the soil but also their
urban cousins; artisans produced more goods than they
could themselves consume; merchants facilitated the
exchange of apples for clothing, wheat for coal, dairy
products for beverages. Assuredly, the services rendered by these several classes did much to promote the
general welfare of society. Smith willingly admitted
that the division of labor had been largely responsible
for the progress of European culture, but the hard-
headed Scotsman refused to confine his interest to the
purely superficial aspects of this development.[4] His
careful studies convinced him that the conduct of the
several classes was not always above reproach, for they
would upon occasion play unfairly, using loaded dice,
which the uninitiated were naturally unable to observe.
Smith was not a little proud of his detective work, for
he hoped that his disclosures would increase the caution and therefore advance the welfare of the naïve
majority. The knavish members of society have known
only too well the best means of enhancing their own
fortunes, but no nation has ever prospered because of
the scrupulousness of the unscrupulous.

The state has frequently granted monopolistic
privileges, but in so doing has directly militated
against the well-being of all who are not members of a
favored association. The price of a monopolized article

will be upon every occasion the highest that can possibly be squeezed out of the buyers.[5] If the government were not to interfere, merchants would sell their wares at more reasonable prices and the public would benefit by being able to purchase its goods more cheaply. The privileges of the merchants and manufacturers enhance the prices which landlords, farmers, and laborers are forced to pay for their goods.[6] The latter have, however, frequently approved the several regulations in restraint of production and trade, though only to suffer later from their own actions. For instance, the granting of a monopoly to the East India Company upon imports from the Far East, resulted in raising the prices of Indian and Chinese goods.[7]

At the beginning of the eighteenth century the Sacred and Royal Majesty of Great Britain signed a reciprocal trade agreement with the King of Portugal. The treaty permitted the import of English woolen goods into Portugal and in return Parliament promised to reduce the tariff on wines from that country to a point below the rates on French vintages. The English manufacturers were indebted to the legislature for the addition of a large market, but Parliament was probably oblivious to the costs of its kindness and consideration. Clearly any tariff, even a differential tariff, made it more expensive for Englishmen to tickle their palates.[8]

The government at the behest of native producers frequently placed very high duties upon foreign goods, and at times even imposed an absolute prohibition upon the import of manufactured commodities. Drastic legislation in favor of the commercial classes was

always certain to prove costly, and less radical measures like the monopolization of colonial trade would
probably also hurt the community. The high profits
which the merchants obtained by controlling the
trade with America, in no way compensated for the increased prices which the landowners were forced to
pay. The laborer likewise suffered from this monopoly
for an excess of funds was employed in colonial trade.
If the merchants' privileges were withdrawn, a redistribution of capital would doubtless take place,
with the result that a larger number of productive
laborers could be supported because the country's
wealth would then be more efficiently invested. The
failure of the government to continue its assistance to
colonial commerce would affect adversely only a small
group of merchants, but would greatly benefit the
large classes of landowners and laborers.

The merchants and manufacturers were not the only
people who pursued their own interests to the disadvantage of the commonwealth's interests. The
laboring groups were guilty to a limited extent of the
same misdemeanor, for the corporations by restricting
the number of apprentices and journeymen enhanced
the wages of the artisans and therefore raised the price
of their wares. The public which suffered from these
restraints could protect itself by declaring all trades
open, for such a policy would doubtless result in increasing competition and lowering prices.

Almost all European countries have obstructed the
free circulation of labor, thereby causing a most inconvenient inequality in the distribution of the working
population.[9] Late in the nineteenth century laborers in

Devon had never heard of Lancashire, although they might have doubled their wages by moving to the latter county. If a large influx had taken place, the wages of the cotton hands would have been depressed to the immediate disadvantage of the older workers.[10] The public, however, would have gained by being able to purchase its cloth more cheaply and the laborers would also have benefited before long from the more efficient distribution of the country's resources.

The farming interest has seldom had an opportunity to gain at the expense of the other classes. Occasionally, an agricultural community possessed a natural monopoly in supplying food products to a neighboring town, but better roads and deeper rivers have made it possible for outlying districts to ship their products to the city. The increase in the supply of agricultural commodities has been of great advantage to the urban population by enabling it to purchase its provisions more cheaply. The landed class has not suffered greatly from the loss of this monopoly; doubtless it receives less for the products of the land, but the land itself has become more valuable.[11]

A tradesman did not always benefit greatly from a monopolistic control of the market. A butcher, because of the absence of competition, was able to charge exorbitant prices for his meat. But if there were only one butcher, there was probably also only one baker. The butcher was therefore forced to overpay for his bread. The public, however, was the greatest loser because it purchased all its commodities at enhanced values.[12]

Monopoly was the great obstacle in the path of the community's progress, for it retarded the advancement of industry and checked the increase in population. The nation's hope lay in the more widespread introduction of competitive conditions.[13] The banking business best illustrates the advantages which would accrue to the public from the destruction of a monopoly. When the notes of only a few large financial houses circulate, their soundness is a cause of constant concern. If a large number of banks were permitted to issue paper, the failure of one or two institutions could not seriously affect the public. Furthermore, the small tradesman would benefit because increased competition would force the several institutions to solicit his trade, thus putting an end to the arrogant dealings of bankers which have been all too frequent in the past.[14]

The state, however, has a perfect right, if it so desires, to place restraints upon the banking business. It is always justifiable to limit the natural liberty of a few individuals if the security of the entire society is thereby enhanced. Governmental action will probably always affect adversely certain people but, as long as it benefits the community at large, one need not become unduly concerned with the incidental losses of a few individuals—especially if they be wealthy and powerful. Injustice is committed only when the fortunes of a small group are advanced at the expense of the general public. The members of society obtain their incomes from the rent of land, from the wages of labor, or from the profits of capital. But the state is more than a simple aggregation of the agricultural, the laboring, and the commercial classes.

The rent of land depends upon the advance of society, and hence landowners ought to be vitally concerned with the promotion of the general welfare. Unfortunately, their wealth does not spring from their own exertions and they are therefore likely to become both indifferent and indolent. Despite these failings, landlords ought to be trusted in all discussions of commercial policy because they can never advance their own fortunes at the expense of the public. They sponsor or support harmful legislation, as in the case of the corn bounty, only when they fail to understand their own position. The grain statute which the country gentry passed in the hope of advancing their own interest turned out to be advantageous only to the small group of corn merchants.[15] A well-informed landed class need never be feared; an ignorant one might prove dangerous.

The interests of the workers cannot conflict with those of society because the demand for labor will increase only when the stock and the revenue of a country are augmented.[16] Wages are closely correlated with the rate of a nation's progress and are always highest in a country which is developing most rapidly. During the eighteenth century America was expanding at a rapid rate, England more moderately, and the empire of the mandarins not at all. Hence the laborer in New York was in a much more enviable position than either the London artisan or the Chinese coolie.

The commercial class which directs in large part the economic processes of a country is the only group which upon occasion has interests divergent from those of society. It derives its income from profits, which are always highest in a backward and lowest in an advanced nation. Merchants and manufacturers are

most concerned with buying cheaply and selling
dearly, while the public is always interested in pur-
chasing its goods at the lowest possible prices. Clearly,
there exists a dissonance between the objectives of
these two orders of men. The commercial class is also
the active supporter of monopolies, because these help
to enhance profits artificially. The public, which
would benefit greatly by the disappearance of these
institutions, is once again at cross-purposes with the
merchants, who often oppress and deceive it.[17]

The mercantile system deliberately sought to promote the interests of the producers by stimulating
native industries. A most superficial consideration
would have illustrated the stupidity of this procedure.
Production for production's sake was meaningless;
goods were useful only because they satisfied the needs
and desires of men. The outstanding error of British
commercial policy was the preferment of the producers. The state in granting the merchants and manufacturers a monopoly of the Irish trade hoped to enrich
the country by increasing the well-being of the commercial classes.[18] The consumers, however, had the
satisfaction of knowing that they were enhancing the
wealth of the already wealthy merchants. They were
furthermore so kindly inclined that they even burdened
themselves with the support of a large over-sea empire
in order to insure the commercial class an outlet for
their products. The sacrifices of the consuming public
were not really appreciated.[19]

The true lovers of English culture often extolled
the successful struggles for liberty which their ancestors had waged. The Glorious Revolution of 1688

was a most decisive victory over despotism. Now, monopolies which had been part of the old autocratic régime should have disappeared at that time, but Englishmen, who were proud of their newly acquired rights and privileges continued to tolerate these institutions. The public acted in good faith, but was narcotized by the soothing principles which the private interests proclaimed.

Corporations with exclusive privileges alone prevented prices from falling and therefore were responsible for the country's slow advance.[20] Few people realized that the law in securing the monopolist from rivals removed the last check upon his ability to practice extortion. The deleterious effect of this protection was most evident when one studied the investments of a monopolist, for he never placed his capital in trades where he was able to earn a fair rate of return, but always concentrated his resources in that one undertaking which assured him extraordinary profits. The government, by increasing the lucrativeness of certain investments, interfered with the maximum efficiency of the economic system, and thereby deprived many thousands of families of employment. The state, in permitting merchants and manufacturers to proceed under cover of the law, prostituted its honor.[21]

The class legislation which Parliament had passed in favor of the commercial interests impeded but could not completely halt the nation's progress. The distinguished French physician and economist, Quesnay, had assumed that a country could thrive only under a regular régime of perfect liberty and perfect justice. Adam Smith knew, however, that Europe had been able to progress despite many bad laws and institutions, though he believed that it was his duty, and the duty of all reformers, to uproot the noxious weeds.[22] He realized that this was no easy task and therefore was careful to appeal not to reason and humanity but to the self-love of his fellow citizens.[23] The legislators at Westminster had frequently acted to their own disadvantage, but had never clearly perceived the costliness of their mistakes. Smith believed that they could be protected against themselves only if they were enlightened as to the machinations of the tricky tradesmen who had pulled the wool over their eyes.[24]

Ever since the Reformation, England had made more rapid progress in politics, law, and economics than had most European countries. During this advance an increasing number of institutions were becoming obsolete. Many persons not only did not realize that these institutions were outmoded, but actually ascribed the country's progress to them.[25] It was one of Adam Smith's outstanding contributions to evaluate carefully the costs of evil in the midst of common good.

The Learned and the Pious

Plato believed that the world would never be perfect until philosophers were kings, and kings philosophers; he therefore looked forward to the day when a race of supermen would inherit the earth. He realized, however, that even in his ideal society the soldiers of the spirit would still have to be housed, clothed, and fed; hence he provided in his constitution for a large group of slaves which would attend to the material needs of the select minority. Plato could not envisage a classless utopia. His realism led him to believe that only a class which possessed wealth and leisure, and was therefore able to devote itself to the cultivation of the spirit, could create a great civilization.

Greece and Rome declined, and Plato's *Republic* was never put to trial. After the fall of the Caesars, the inhabitants of Europe were forced to strain every nerve and fiber in the fierce struggle for survival. For many years the outcome was far from certain. During this period the leaders of society were unable to evidence any pronounced interest in the education of the masses, whose instruction was limited to the more important biblical narratives, and the essential prayers. This modicum of instruction made it possible for the ignorant farmer to appreciate his priest's sermons on the beauties of heaven and the torments of hell. It was neither essential nor desirable that his learning

should exceed these limits, for the Church believed
in the dictum of the sage, "that he who increases
knowledge increases suffering."[1] The ecclesiastical
authorities therefore carefully avoided enlightening
the public for fear of increasing the already limitless
group of human difficulties. They themselves, however,
tempted the devil by not being able to refrain from
scholastic debate. The early disputants were bothered
by such intangible considerations as the number of
angels that could stand on the point of a needle,
though it was not very long before they became
interested in more mundane problems. Soon academies
were established throughout western Europe. At
first theology had a monopoly of the curriculum,
but law, philosophy, and medicine finally broke
down its intrenched position. At the time of the
Reformation, the universities of Paris, Vienna, Prague,
Heidelberg, Bologna, and Oxford were important cultural centers which housed distinguished scientists
and scores of students.

The advancement in learning during the later
Middle Ages did not greatly affect the common people
for they were no more able to read the writings of
Martin Luther than their ancestors had been able to
read the writings of St. Augustine. However, with the
breakdown of feudalism and the economic progress
which followed in its wake, the mode of life of many
was radically altered. Urban centers increased in number and in size; large masses of the country folk took
up residence in the towns. A new industrial and commercial civilization developed. An ignorant population had been viewed with favor by the medieval

Church because it lent stability to the society of the time, but during the commercial revolution it was found to be a great bane, for there were many trades which could not be conducted by illiterates.

The progress of popular education was speeded by the invention of printing, though it received its greatest propulsion from the religious revolt of the northern countries. The Mother Church during the period of its ascendency had led its children along the straight and narrow path, and had not permitted them to engage in any explorations without the guidance of the clergy. The Reformation, however, shifted the emphasis; the individual became largely responsible for saving his own soul. The reading of the Scriptures could alone help men to discover the good life. In medieval times the Church had permitted the populace to read only a strictly censored version of the Bible, and actually preferred that the Holy Book should not be read at all. In the Protestant countries, however, the church service was based upon the Old and New Testaments, and no word in the Holy Writ was unimportant. The schooling of the masses became therefore one of the primary objectives of modern reformers.

At the beginning of the eighteenth century the religious enthusiasm associated with the rebellion against Catholicism had almost completely subsided, for people were becoming increasingly conscious of their pocketbooks and more indifferent to their souls. The public was still vitally concerned with educational problems but not so much with their religious as with their economic and political implications.[2]

The state, though many in the upper classes objected strenuously, had undertaken to support charity schools in which the rudiments of arithmetic and spelling were taught to the children of the laboring poor. The critics rehabilitated in modern dress Plato's thesis of the impracticability of creating a classless society, because they feared that it was unwise for the state wilfully to diminish the numbers of people who currently performed menial tasks. There was no reason to instruct a chimney-sweep or dung collector in reading and writing, for their schooling would not enable them to execute their work more efficiently, and could only make them dissatisfied with their occupations. Widespread discontent among the lower orders might have the most serious repercussions upon the general economic system, for the educated plebeians would try to raise themselves in the social and economic scale, thereby increasing the competition for better positions such as clerkships and bookkeepers' posts. But the offspring of the poor had no right to such employment, because charity schools were supported in large part by taxes upon the middle classes, whose own children held clerical positions. People of moderate circumstances by supporting the education of the poor directly militated against the future success of their own offspring.

The reformers were rather frightened by the potency of these arguments and beat a hasty retreat, in which they sacrificed their ultimate objective in the hope of securing at least part of their gains. They admitted that they did not approve of an extended educational program for the poor, and believed that only an

exceptional child ought to be encouraged.[3] Furthermore, they argued that the poor and insufficient instruction which the children of the laborers received
in the charity schools could never make them worthy
competitors for better positions. The benign paternalism which was practiced in economic spheres was
reflected in the prevailing attitude toward education.[4]

A marked difference of opinion existed concerning
the political expediency of educating the masses.
Many were of the opinion that the security of the state
would be enhanced if the laboring poor were kept illiterate. Others, pointing out that vice and iniquity
were practiced more freely by the unlearned than by
the schooled, argued that the state and private property would be more nearly invulnerable if the working
class were educated.[5] On these disputed issues, Adam
Smith took a most radical position. He advocated the
widespread dissemination of learning because he believed education to offer the weaker classes one of the
most efficient instruments for their own improvement.
There was nothing sacrosanct in the existing class relations. The difference between a philosopher and a
common street porter could be explained by habit,
custom, and education; during childhood, there is
little to distinguish the future sage from the common
laborer.[6] Environmental forces permit the talents of
one to develop, while they stifle the native abilities of
the other.[7] Society and not nature makes men.

The laboring poor suffer greatly from their lack of
education because in the economic struggle between
the classes they are unable properly to further their
own interests.[8] The community need never fear the

ambition of the working population, for it will always benefit from the exertion of people to better their own positions. An industrious and prosperous working class is the greatest boon to the welfare of a nation, and only a petty group could desire to keep laborers ignorant in order to safeguard its own economic interests.[9]

The development of commerce and industry which has done so much to increase the happiness of mankind has had a most unfortunate influence upon the mentality of the populace. The division of labor, which has been largely responsible for economic progress, has made it necessary for many a man to be occupied during the entire working day with the performance of the most minute operation. The common people in a rich industrial community are more stupid than those in a poor agricultural district.[10] Clearly a man who spends his life in tightening screws has little occasion to sharpen his intelligence or improve his understanding. He is likely to sink to the lowest level of stupidity and ignorance.[11]

In Scotland the meanest porter can read and write because even the very poor can afford the meager costs of schooling. Furthermore, the children of the laboring classes can find no employment until they reach their teens and hence their parents are not tempted to exploit them. This is not the case in certain parts of England, where a child of six or seven can earn a few pence per day, and is more frequently sent to work than to school. The potential earning power of the young has most unfortunate consequences, for a lad who has never learnt to employ his mind is forced to rely for relaxation upon the stimulation of his senses. Workmen in the industrial sections of England are often in a despicable condition for they pass much of their time in drunkenness and riot. Their debauched state, however, might never have resulted, had they received in their youth even the most elementary education.[12]

The inability of the ignorant laborer to form judgments on issues of public concern makes him an amenable tool in the hands of unscrupulous agitators. The enthusiasms and superstitions of the populace have frequently led to the most dreadful disorders, and it would be greatly to the advantage of the state to offer its members at least a minimum of instruction in order to safeguard itself against violent outbursts. An intelligent people is especially important in a free nation where public opinion plays a significant rôle.[13]

An uneducated workman is dangerous to the state because he is incapable of forming judgments about the ordinary problems of his own life. A free society will never survive unless the general population can be trusted to take care of itself. A man who has passed his childhood without any schooling, and whose trade in later life does not permit him to make good this deficiency, is certain to be a worthless citizen. Not knowing how else to spend his leisure, he will doubtless engage in riotous amusements, and dissipate his resources. It would be wise for him to save and invest his surplus earnings or else expend them in training himself for a more lucrative trade; but unfortunately he does neither.

The state is becoming more industrialized every day and it must be on its guard against the complete corruption and degeneration of the great body of the people. The government is not confronted with so serious a problem in agricultural communities because the many activities in which a farmer engages will prevent him from succumbing to mental lethargy. The problem, however, is both serious and urgent when one considers the urban laborer.[14]

The education of the common people should concern the public much more than the training of the wealthier classes, for people of rank and fortune do not enter upon a career until the end of their teens, and will never devote their entire time to their work. The round of activities in which the rich engage makes it unreasonable to fear that their understanding will grow torpid from lack of exercise. The opposite is true when one considers the masses, for they are forced to earn their living early in life, and therefore the time and money expended on their instruction must be carefully controlled. The state should facilitate, encourage, and even impose the essentials of learning upon the large body of the people by establishing schools in every district, where the children of the poor would be taught to read and write. The expenses entailed by a general educational program could well be met by general taxation, for society at large would benefit from a more literate population.

Teachers are underpaid and their profession is degraded from its status in past ages. The public, however, is benefited by this inequality, for a cheapening in the cost of schooling can never prove inconvenient.

Unfortunately the schoolmaster's lot is not a happy one, for his pupils' fees are seldom sufficient to prevent him from starving, and he is therefore frequently forced to clerk or slave in order to eke out a living. If a young man is seeking a genteel profession, he should by all means avoid a position in a school, for seven years' apprenticeship at a cutler's wheel would be more pleasant; and even Newgate Prison compares favorably with many an educational institute.

Despite the unenviable position of the schoolmaster, some might fear that he would neglect his duties if the state paid him a regular salary, and would therefore prefer that he be supported by the tuition monies of his pupils. There is a widespread opinion that all salaried officials have a tendency to malinger and that they will perform the requisite quantity and quality of work only if their rewards are made to depend upon their exertions.

The school curriculum should be radically revised, because it fails completely to serve the needs of the students. Children should read about animals and flowers rather than fairies and elves. It would be much more to the point to teach a lad who plans to enter the carpentering or the iron trade the essentials of physics and geometry rather than the declensions of Latin nouns. He would not only be more interested in the scientific subjects and therefore learn more rapidly, but he might actually find them useful in his later work.

The education of the middle classes is also in urgent need of reform, for at present youths who plan to enter trade are kept busy learning dead languages. The stupidity of such instruction becomes clear if one compares it to the upbringing of Jewish children, who are taught early in life, modern languages and the principles of business. While the one group is worried about the syntax of a Greek word, the other is already engaged upon the successful direction of financial undertakings. The useless pedantry to which the youths of our public schools are subjected cannot possibly be defended.[15]

The education of girls is quite bad. At boarding schools they are taught in great detail the amenities of social intercourse and behavior, without ever receiving the slightest instruction in domestic economy. After marriage they are unable to manage their homes efficiently and their husbands cannot trust them with the purse strings because they have never been taught the value of money. In short, their schooling has been as deficient as that of their brothers.[16]

The state can doubtless influence the education of the masses; it will find it more difficult to interfere with the education of the bourgeoisie. In order to raise the general level of the community, the several municipalities should require all tradesmen and journeymen to undergo an examination before they are granted permission to settle and pursue their occupations.[17] If necessary, the state should use its political and economic powers to force a minimum of education upon the general public.

The most complex of all educational problems is the improvement in the schooling of the rich. The universities have long been the very backbone of the educational system of the country and have been responsible in no small part for the progress of the nation's culture. The schools of higher learning have accumulated during the centuries very substantial endowments which have exercised a most important influence upon their general development.[18] A discussion of universities must commence with a consideration of their funded wealth. Upon analysis, one discovers that endowments have not facilitated the dissemination of knowledge, nor increased the diligence of the pupils, nor enhanced the brilliance of the faculty. The economic security of the teaching staff has had a most baneful influence, because the instructors realize that they will eat and be clothed irrespective of the quality of their work.[19] Man is naturally indolent. For a long time the professors at Oxford have given up even the pretence of teaching.[20]

The curriculum is centuries out of date, for few changes have been introduced since the time when monks and priests controlled the destinies of the universities.[21] Modern discoveries have made the philosophy and science of the Middle Ages largely anachronistic, but Oxford, and to a lesser degree Cambridge, have completely ignored these intellectual revolutions. They have remained sanctuaries for exploded systems and obsolete prejudices.[22] Their entrenched wealth has made it possible for them to take no account of world opinion and they are not in the least disturbed that an able and ambitious young man, after pursuing a course of studies for several years within their portals, might still be completely ignorant of the most important and pressing problems of the day.[23]

During the Middle Ages all subjects of university instruction were subservient to theology, and the scholastic harangues of the clergy were organized into systematic courses. In ancient times the philosophers were less interested in problems of the supernatural; their disquisitions centered upon human institutions. What was the best political organization? What changes should be introduced to improve the family? Could man be taught to lead a nobler life? The medieval temper had no use for these questions; ascetic morality was eminently superior to pragmatic ethics. Subtlety and sophistry were the principal contributions of the scholastics to the development of philosophy. The understanding of men was, however, not greatly improved by disputing the number of wings of the cherubim nor the punishments which a sinner would receive in the hereafter. Unfortunately many universities still occupy themselves with these subjects, but even these problems are badly presented by lazy instructors.

The educational policies of the universities which set up metaphysics in opposition to physics are most ill founded, for little can ever be learnt about the questions with which metaphysics professes to deal. The cultivation of this branch of learning increases obscurities and uncertainties without leading to any tangible results. If the universities were to focus their attention upon experimentation and observation, the value of their instruction would be greatly enhanced. Physics, that most useful science, has made great progress because of the methods which it employs, and it is as ill-judged to avoid instructing the gentry's sons in this useful discipline as it is to teach the children of the common people Latin.

Adam Smith, though he spent six years at Oxford, profited little from his sojourn. At Glasgow he concentrated upon mathematics; at Oxford he specialized in languages. It is not impossible that considerations of expediency forced him to forego his first love; he doubtless decided, after discovering that teachers did not teach at Oxford, that he could make better progress under his own tutelage in literature and philosophy than in mathematics.[24]

Smith spent some fifteen years at Glasgow as both student and professor, and upon the basis of this experience came to the conclusion that the Scottish universities, despite their many shortcomings, were the best seminaries of learning in all of Europe. His criticism of Oxford, however, was not entirely due to the poor figure which the English institution cut beside the Scottish college; Oxford was absolutely, not relatively, poor. Gibbon concurred whole-heartedly with Smith in this evaluation of the English university; the distinguished historian called the fourteen months which he spent at Oxford the most idle and unprofitable period in his entire life.[25] That eccentric genius, Jeremy Bentham, was of like opinion; he maintained that nothing could possibly be learned at Oxford.[26]

Smith was never purely destructive for, no matter how devastating his criticism might be, he was always certain to offer suggestions for reform. He practiced what he taught, moral philosophy! Gibbon believed that the monopoly which the universities enjoyed was, like all monopolies, narrow, lazy, and oppressive; Smith agreed with him and therefore advocated as the first step in his program of reform the immediate abolition of certain arbitrary regulations which had long been in force. Pupils who held scholarships, exhibitions, and bursaries were attached to one of the several colleges without any consideration being paid to their own wishes, for clearly beggars could not be choosers. If this precedent were abolished, the colleges would be forced to compete, and the resulting emulation would doubtless raise the standards of instruction.[27]

In the past the discipline of the colleges was contrived not for the benefit of the students but for the convenience of the instructors. An indifferent teacher could lecture with great pomp and solemnity upon a subject of which he knew little and cared less, and the students were compelled to attend and to listen. The professor could insure himself against all trouble by translating from a foreign book or by the even easier method of requiring one of his students to do so. The performance would be highly decent and respectable, but clearly worthless.

The university authorities frequently accused the student body of being depraved, while at the same time they exalted the wisdom and learning of the faculty. It was false, however, to maintain that the vicious nature of young men led them to despise either their instructors or their instruction. Students were sensitive, especially sensitive to inferior teachers and teaching, but they were also appreciative of and responsive to stimulating instruction.

If the education of youth had remained entirely upon a private basis, the quality of teaching would doubtless have been much better, for a pedagogue could then have obtained pupils only by virtue of his reputation. He would not have dared force his unfortunate victims to swallow the pretentious claptrap of bygone ages, because his livelihood would have depended upon the public's evaluation of his worth.

The great improvements in science and philosophy have not been made within the wealthy universities: the most important cultural contributions have been produced by scholars in smaller institutions. Many scientists worked hard to establish their reputations and modernize their opinions and beliefs because their income depended almost entirely upon fees; and this progressiveness of the smaller universities gave them a decided advantage over the heavily endowed institutions.[28]

During the eighteenth century it was quite common for children of the rich, in their late teens and early twenties, to travel on the Continent. Clearly this custom could never have become well established, had not the universities fallen to a very low depth. No one was willing to believe that his children could learn less in Paris than in Oxford. Actually, the young gentlemen would gain little by their Continental jaunt: they might acquire a smattering of one or two foreign languages, but would probably master only the art of dissipated living.[29]

The educational system of the British Isles resembled in many respects the economic organization of the country. The large universities were not unlike the powerful, exclusive companies; the smaller colleges were a counterpart of the newer trades which depended for their existence not upon privileges but upon the intrinsic quality of their merchandise; the private teacher was confronted with the same problems as the independent artisan.

Adam Smith evidenced the same reforming tendencies in education as in economics, for in both he was primarily interested in improving society by strengthening the weaker class. His methods, however, differed. At one time he advocated increasing the scope of governmental activity, while at another he desired to restrain the state from undue interference. Smith was willing to employ all means to enhance social welfare as long as they did not prove more costly than the ends attained.

Traffic in souls competed with traffic in wheat. During the centuries when the Holy Roman Church dominated Europe, there existed little opportunity for any institution to escape the supervision of the clergy. Now it happened that the Church was not greatly interested in abetting the people's accumulation of wealth or knowledge, because it believed that both economic and intellectual progress, though not bad for itself, were not good for the populace. The papacy could not entirely neglect the economic status of its charges, for the contributions of the faithful were of great importance in sustaining the power of the priestly hierarchy. The Church, however, showed instinctive good judgment when it failed to encourage business enterprise; it feared that an enhancement in the wealth of the people would have an unfavorable reaction upon its own welfare. It needed money but it was not willing to risk upsetting the social and economic world to obtain it.

Despite the resistance of the Church, the commercial revolution occurred. Now it was not long before the faithful, though possessed of greater wealth, reduced their scale of oblations. The peoples of the north commenced to employ accounting methods in their daily business life, which meant that they carefully balanced costs against profits. There was no certainty that, having acquired this habit, they would act otherwise on Sundays than on week days. The rich Florentine cities could not be coerced into generous support of the Vatican; nor could the prosperous Low Countries be taxed heavily; England, likewise, was not a financial bulwark of the Church of Rome. The Church in the years preceding the Reformation had engaged in many dubious practices; the dissipation of the spiritual heads of the Church had commenced to disgust thoughtful people.[30] If the books of the ecclesiastical organization were ever audited, the insolvency of the corporation could probably no longer be kept from the general public. In England, the power of the Catholic Church was, however, destroyed before the audit took place.

Rome interfered with the sex life of a king, the social life of the upper classes, and the business life of the bourgeoisie. The obtrusion was not great, but nevertheless sufficient to be unpleasant. England rid itself of Romanism. Thereafter business boomed and not a few observers ascribed the rising prosperity to the schism.[31] The economic progress of Great Britain

could probably be accounted for more easily by
changes in the material than in the spiritual realm.
Protestantism was perhaps more the result than the
cause of the commercial revolution: the stomach spoke
to the soul, rather than the soul to the stomach.[32]

British writers long after the Reformation maintained that Catholicism was the worst enemy of national prosperity; they were constantly proving to
their own satisfaction that the misery of Ireland resulted from the Popish religion. The Anglican economists felt certain that the poverty of Ireland was due
to the large number of religious holidays, for clearly
the Catholic religion hindered trade if it prevented the
laborer from working during a third of the year. In
ascribing the superiority of England to Protestantism,
they completely overlooked the fact that Parliament
constantly stifled Irish commerce.[33]

The eighteenth century, despite its liberalism,
never ceased to fear the Church of Rome; even the
enlightened author of *Tom Jones*, in one of his books,
coupled Popish priests with common rogues and
bandits.[34] The educated members of society distrusted
Catholicism because they feared that they might be
deprived of their liberties if the priesthood regained
its power.[35]

Adam Smith was much less frightened by the
priests than most Britons, though he considered the
Church during the period of its ascendancy to have
been the most formidable combination which was ever
arrayed against the civil authority. The liberty, reason, and happiness of mankind had doubtless suffered
during that period, but now the ecclesiastical suze-

rainty was clearly on the decline; in fact it would not be surprising if, within the next few centuries, it were to become completely impotent.[36]

Smith was much more critical of Protestantism than of Catholicism, because the Kirk dominated his own religious environment. He felt rather well inclined toward Catholicism because whatever might be said against the Roman priests they never ceased to tend their flocks. In fact, the mendicant orders, because they depended entirely upon the oblations of the people, were frequently overzealous in preaching the gospel.[37]

The spiritual leaders of the Church of England stood in an entirely different relationship to the public for like most university professors, they lived upon benefices. Inasmuch as they received their bread and butter from the rich, they threw in their lot with the ruling classes and withdrew themselves from any intimate contact with the populace. Their influence with the masses was slight. Now the success of the Methodist revival could be explained in no small measure by the directness and poignancy of Wesley's appeal. Educated people had good reason to fear this movement because it appealed to fanaticism. It must be said to the credit of the Anglican ministry that it looked askance at spiritual excesses, and placed a high value upon learning and culture.

Smith had personal grounds for appreciating the unpleasantness of overzealous souls, for during his Glasgow days the fervent Presbyterians had constantly scrutinized his theological beliefs and utterances. His friendship with Hume was a priori evidence of his

heterodox views. It was even gossiped that he smiled
in chapel and petitioned the college senate to dispense
with the opening prayer in his classes. The fanaticism
of the orthodox groups became so intense that Smith
had to enlist the aid of a prominent lord to still the
charges of heresy which they leveled against him.[38]
It is surprising that his religious opinions became the
subject of suspicion because he was by nature rather
shrewd and cautious in his dealings with his fellow
men. He would never deliberately antagonize a hostile
audience. However, the conservative clergy of the
eighteenth century would doubtless have attacked
even the orthodoxy of Calvin.

Hume had been damned early in life, and the growing intimacy of Smith with the heretic convinced the
public that the economist was as much an atheist as
the philosopher. Upon the death of Hume, Smith had
occasion to write a very beautiful letter in which he
praised the noble character of his late friend.[39] This
epistle became public and the defenders of religion immediately began to attack Smith: no good Christian
could possibly praise Hume. The president of an Oxford College took it upon himself publicly to chastise
Smith, who now, upon his own testimony, stood convicted.[40] The Scottish economist was startled to find
himself the target for clerical criticism; the public's
reaction to his letter took him completely unaware.
His experiences early in life with the Glasgow Presbyterians had reinforced his cautiousness in matters of
religion, and he carefully avoided any overt acts which
could possibly give offense. For instance, David Hume
left in manuscript his *Dialogues concerning Natural*

Religion which he hoped would see the light of day after his death; but Smith, though literary executor, refused to associate himself in any respect with the publication of this work, because he feared the public clamor which would be raised against such an ir-religious tract. The book was printed, but it failed to cause any disturbance. Smith's caution had proved excessive.[41]

Several years later, Smith again thought it wise to tread lightly in the field of religious controversy. A friend who had written a book against the austerity of the Scottish Sabbath asked his advice about publication. They both agreed that the Scriptures did not prescribe a Puritanical rest day, but Smith pointed out that it was not solely a question of textual inter-pretation. The Sabbath had a political and social significance which made it inadvisable to suggest radical alterations so long as the majority of the population were conservatively inclined.[42]

Smith, basing his analysis upon his own experi-ence, pointed out in the *Wealth of Nations* that the church became troublesome and dangerous only when one or, at the most, a few sects were tolerated. Monop-oly spiritual is likely to be as oppressive as monopoly material. If several hundred groups were forced to ob-tain and hold adherents, there would be little possi-bility of establishing a powerful ecclesiastical institu-tion, and an alliance between the civil and the reli-gious authorities would be still more difficult. The many sects would be forced to tolerate and respect one an-other, thus holding popular superstition and enthusi-asm in check.[43]

The division of society into classes on the basis of economic wealth frequently results in a bifurcation of religious systems; the common people generally adhere to an austere and rigorous morality, while the wealthier groups tend toward a more liberal code. Economic forces determine this difference. If a poor man were to engage in the dissipations of the rich, they would almost inevitably lead to his swift and sudden ruin. On the other hand it is not impossible for a man of rank to survive the ill effects of a much looser life. The partisans of the austere systems frequently object to the mirth, folly, and extravagance which are countenanced by the more liberal orders. The religious and moral fervor of the conservatives is apt, however, to become upon occasion distinctly disagreeable and unsocial. This is especially true if the populace succumbs to the spell of a powerful leader.[44]

The state should combat fanaticism by encouraging the study of science and philosophy, which are excellent antidotes to enthusiasm and superstition. The government could achieve this end by requiring all prospective members of the liberal professions to undergo examinations in these subjects. If the upper classes were free from dogmatism, there would be less chance for the common people to become a prey to its ravages. The community could also exert its influence most effectively by encouraging all types of public diversions. Dancing, music, and especially dramatic performances should be sponsored by the public authority for, if the common people could be amused and pleased, they would be less given to fanatical exuberance.[45]

Religion has had a tremendous hold upon men because it exploited their instinct of fear.[46] The priests by their pictures of everlasting damnation have kept the population in awe of their spiritual authority. The clergy in order to strengthen their control over the lives of men have generally refused to compromise, demanding from the members of their church an absolute adherence to the entire body of dogma. The singleness of purpose of the incorporated body of ecclesiastics has always reacted unfavorably upon the welfare of the state, and the public would gain greatly from a disruption of this monopoly. Much of the absurdity, imposture, and fanaticism which are at present attached to religious doctrines could be eradicated if there were many small sects instead of a few powerful institutions. A pure and rational religion would then result, and this is what philosophers of all ages have always desired.

The great wealth of a church does not prove its worth, for in most cases it reflects only the poverty of the people.[47] The most successful form of religious organization has been developed in Scotland and Switzerland where there exists an equality of authority and benefice among the Calvinistic clergy. These ministers are both learned and moral; moreover, they always remain in close contact with the people of their parishes. Their salaries are not large, but this fact is more a blessing than a curse. Wealth has always been the great corruptor of human institutions. Money has never made the learned more learned, nor the pious more pious.

A Better World for All

Books beget books; books beget actions. They can amuse and they can teach. Now their educative, reforming interest has not been of like intensity throughout the ages. It reached a high point in the eighteenth century. The drive was especially strong in France, where a corrupt government oppressed the masses. The intellectuals who were responsible for the subversive propaganda were, as could be expected, molested by the censor because he well realized that no good could come of their rantings.[1]

The literati did not play with matches without realizing the dangers of fire, although they were doubtless surprised at the size of the conflagration which broke out in 1789. Their success was greater than they themselves desired. During the eighteenth century conditions in England were not so unpleasant and depressing as in France, for the Germans who sat upon the throne in Buckingham Palace were not strong enough to be truly annoying. When George III finally permitted his nerves to get the best of him and commenced to act like a prima donna, many in the audience left, while others remained to engage in disrespectful whistling. Continental tricksters were not highly appreciated in England; rather the reverse.

Voltaire, the leader of the Enlightenment, was especially well liked by English liberals, and Adam

Smith's regard for the famous critic was most pronounced. The bonds of communion between the product of Scottish Presbyterianism and Gallic Catholicism must never be overlooked in the interpretation of these two very different geniuses. For instance, Smith pointed out that in the past grave philosophers have written many tomes, but few have taken the trouble to read them. However, the writings of Voltaire, which have made the lives of fanatics miserable, are read by all; hence the world has benefited more from this one essayist than from all the other subtle metaphysicians. Smith had greater respect for Voltaire than for any other living man. During his European trip, he traveled to Geneva with the young Duke of Buccleugh in order to be in the company of the French author, who was then living on the shores of Lake Leman.[2]

Adam Smith admired another man, a native of Geneva, who was in only a slightly lesser degree than Voltaire responsible for the Bourbons losing their throne. Though Smith at one time called Jean Jacques Rousseau a great rascal and a hypocritical pedant, he was not blind to Rousseau's contributions to the cause of reform.[3] Smith once remarked that the *Social Contract* would one day avenge all the persecutions which its author had suffered.[4]

Paris, prior to the Revolution, though it could boast of but one Voltaire and one Rousseau, was nevertheless remarkably rich in talented people. The large circle of scientists, philosophers, and economists who frequented the salons formed one of the most important groups in contemporary French society. A foreigner like Hume was most impressed with these

intellectuals, and they were also sufficiently cosmopolitan to appreciate the Scottish genius.[5] Hume
was ignored in his own country except by the
clergy who attacked his atheism, but in France his
praise was loudly sung.[6] Adam Smith was also in
close spiritual contact with this circle, for one of its
members supervised the translation of his *Theory of
Moral Sentiments*.[7] Despite the differences between the
cultures on opposite shores of the Channel, the friendship between French and English intellectuals was not
difficult to understand. They had a common interest in
reforming the societies in which they lived and,
though their specific objectives differed, their methods
were very similar. The Continental and Island liberals
were both forced to use the pen as their principal
weapon of attack; they were brothers in arms fighting
for the same cause under different banners.

Smith at various times in his life illustrated his
attitude and approach to problems of social reform.
His predecessors at Glasgow had taught their pupils
much logic and metaphysics, but he believed that it
was preferable to direct the attention of young
scholars to more interesting and practical disciplines.[8]
Furthermore, Smith in his lectures on economics,
pointed out the great advantages of using the art of
persuasion in social struggles, which he believed
could be most effectively developed by appealing to
the self-love of one's fellow men.[9] He advised all reformers not to neglect this valuable instrument.[10]
Obviously, there is nothing naïve about Smith. He
was amused by the pedantry of Gallic philosophers,[11]
and in fact criticised Turgot because that statesman

had failed to discount the selfishness, the stupidity, and the prejudice which prevailed in the world. Dugald Stewart, Smith's first biographer, relates that the Scottish professor was wont to treat economic problems in terms of expediency rather than of justice;[12] nor was he likely to underestimate the cupidity of mankind, for when he erred it was on the side of discounting the forces for good. During the fifties, the Chair of Logic became vacant at Glasgow, and Smith writes that he would prefer David Hume to any other man for this position; the public, however, was not of like opinion, and he felt that popular prejudice must be respected.[13] Any attempt to run counter to a widespread bias would end in dismal failure, illustrating nothing more than the infantile mind of the venturous individual.

The *Wealth of Nations* was written by one who might well be called a practical idealist, for Smith did believe that many improvements could be introduced into the social structure. But any reform, no matter how well intentioned, was certain to be stillborn, if the advocate failed to consider the attitudes of the people with whom he dealt. Smith was too keen a student of human nature to believe that radical measures could be successful if they ran counter to the prevailing psychological outlook.

Mercantilistic England, or what remained of high mercantilism in the eighteenth century, was thoroughly disliked by Adam Smith. The privileges of the merchants and manufacturers had been unfairly obtained and were now being unfairly maintained. Of late the landlords had attempted to imitate the shrewd and crafty tradesmen in the hope of securing important benefits from the system, and even the laborers in certain corporations had secured the power to fleece the public for their private advantage. The exploitation of the population by special interests was most unfortunate, and any system which permitted, and in fact encouraged such thievery was clearly unworthy of respect. Unfortunately, the corruption was not confined to the economic realm; political life had also become diseased.

The liberties of Englishmen had been gained only after a slow and laborious struggle. But in the eighteenth century the British Isles were, with the possible exception of the Netherlands, the most liberal country in Europe. Paris might be the cultural center of western civilization, and a most pleasant city in which to reside so long as one did not annoy the officers of His Majesty, the King of France. If for any reason one were so unlucky as to come under the surveillance of the police, his days and nights became one long trial and tribulation. It was David Hume, disliked by Whig and Tory, by Scotsman and Englishman, by members of the established and the independent churches, who advised Rousseau to settle in England because of the superior guarantees of individual freedom under the Georges.[14] The increasing emancipation of the English citizenry from the shackles of political restraints was especially valued by men who knew the story of the past struggles; and Smith's dislike of the existing mercantilistic system was in no small measure predicated upon his unwillingness to countenance any interference with the progress of governmental reform. He was much perturbed by the limitations upon the mobility of the laboring population, the restrictions upon engaging in business, and the broad powers of the excise officials. If they were continued, the liberties of Englishmen would soon be nothing more than a childhood dream. The state neglected the education of the young in order to insure the manufacturing interest a cheap labor supply; in fact the economic nationalism which knew no bounds did not hesitate to weaken directly the fiber of the people. Blame for the prevalence of religious fanaticism could likewise be laid upon the state because it had failed to raise the standards of the working class.

At Toulouse time hung heavily on Smith's hands and he therefore commenced to write on economics, but it was not until twelve years later that the *Wealth of Nations* appeared. During this period he analyzed the materials which demonstrated the disadvantages of permitting the existing economic system to remain unaltered. He painted the society of the future in bright colors, for he well appreciated the problem which confronted him. Nothing could be gained by preaching of a new and better world in the abstract; nor would it be wise to rely upon the insight and understanding of the masses. Religious prophets have often implored the populace to cease sinning and to mend its ways. Jeremiah on the steps of the Temple harangued the multitude because it had renounced Jehovah, but he made little progress by appealing to their moral conscience. To change the attitudes of the people, threats or inducements were necessary. Jeremiah warned the Hebrews that a wrathful God would wreak his vengeance upon them unless they speedily repented. Paul's stressing of immortality accomplished what Jesus' gospel of love had failed to do —the task of converting the pagan world.

Man is most concerned with his own fortunes and misfortunes, and therefore Adam Smith addressed himself to the instinct of self-love in his audience.[15] There is no use in flying in the face of common truths and affirming that man has a highly developed sense of social responsibility. The constant reference to the individual in the economic analysis of the *Wealth of Nations* has pertinency only if one clearly appreciates the author's approach. Smith realizes that his program of reform has no chance of adoption unless it is skillfully maneuvered, and he therefore proceeds most circumspectly. His attack upon mercantilism is so directed as to impress the populace with the losses which it suffers from the existing system, and to illustrate the benefits which it would derive by reforming the existing economic organization. Smith appreciates the fact that he cannot appeal to the private interest of every individual, and he is quite willing to antagonize small minorities so long as he has the support of the majority. The removal of tariffs would lessen the profits of native manufacturers, but benefit all other classes; now Smith feels that if the landlords, the farmers, and the laborers were to act in concert, he need not fear the opposition of the disgruntled producers.

The levity and inconsistency of human nature make the appeal to the self-love of an individual far from foolproof.[16] A laborer would be greatly benefited if, upon finding himself in a locality where low wages prevailed, he removed to a region where workers were more liberally rewarded. But man is queer; he will seldom exert himself even if he can profit greatly by his efforts. Another serious defect in human nature is man's overweening conceit.[17] The readiness with which people gamble, overvaluing the chances for gain and discounting the possibilities of losses, proves the prevalence of self-confidence.[18] The interest of the public in speculative undertakings, where the probability of winning is slight, can likewise be explained by the absurd faith that all men have in their own good fortune. People in planning their daily lives frequently permit their unstable emotions to force sober reason and experience into the background.

A most cursory survey of human psychology would prove that no great reliance should be placed upon the individual, even when he is supposed to act in his own behalf. But despite this knowledge of the frailty of the human flesh and spirit one might advocate a policy of laissez faire in economic and social relations which would still further increase the scope of individual initiative. If the existing economic organization were founded on privilege and supported by restraint, the introduction of widespread freedom into industrial and commercial life might lead to improvements, although one could not be certain that all the evils of the old system would suddenly vanish. State interference with economic enterprise has led to great inequalities; the cessation of governmental intervention might reestablish some degree of equilibrium. A change from an autocratic to a democratic organization of economic society might raise new difficulties in solving old ones. One need but remember that banking companies have evidenced such a lack of appreciation for their own and the public's interest that they have issued many more notes than the community was able to absorb.[19] It is extremely doubtful whether any system of human relations will ever be completely efficient; the advantages of one social order as opposed to another are always relative, never absolute.

The attempt of a central authority to regulate private business is always presumptuous and impertinent, for kings and ministers are most frequently unable to take proper care of their own households.[20] If mistakes in business policy are to be made, the individual entrepreneur is likely to make less serious ones than a bureaucrat in the employ of the government.[21]

The evidence against the good judgment of individuals is almost as considerable as the blunders which could be charged against governments. Esau bartered away his valuable birthright for a bowl of pottage, and many individuals as well as groups have acted in an equally shortsighted manner. Toward the end of the Middle Ages the feudal lords destroyed their own power and authority for a few mean and sordid vanities. Much later, the Bank of England, one of the most influential of all corporations was seen to mistake its own interest. In France, the attitude of the crown and of the populace in matters of taxation was most foolish, for the king and his subjects both worked against their own interest, the one by making vicious demands, the other by feigning poverty to avoid them. The court's income would have been much greater if the exactions had been less onerous, and the people would have been much richer if instead of playing hide and seek with the revenue officers they had exerted all of their energies in the production of wealth.

Men have frequently failed to recognize the mistakes of a policy upon which they have once embarked. A search for gold and silver mines has been under way for many thousands of years. Many hardships have been endured and many lives sacrificed in this crusade, but it has really been a foolish quest. The yellow and the white metals have added little to the happiness of the world. Luxury goods have been cheapened by the abundant supply of gold and silver, and man has been able to indulge his esthetic interests more easily. The moderately rich have eaten from silver platters and the wives of the petty bourgeoisie have bedecked themselves with golden trinkets. No nation, however, has become truly wealthy through the ownership of mines, though its population has perhaps more easily satisfied its desires for frivolous ornamentation.

At certain periods it becomes possible for a nation to raise its standard of living a rung or two by stimulating its industry and its commerce. When this occurs, an excess of coin is customarily found within the borders of the country. At the same time it is not unlikely that the vanity and ostentation of the rich will lead them to add to their precious belongings.

Now although they might invest their excess income in trade, they will probably send it abroad to purchase foreign luxuries. Consumption is doubtless the ultimate end of man's exertions and the expenditure of the rich might at first glance seem justifiable. This is a poor world. It is therefore most important that funds which are able to support the laboring poor by furthering productive industry should not be dissipated. Capital, even excess capital, must be carefully conserved. The prodigal who spends more than his income is most dangerous to society; and the idle, by diminishing the funds which support productive labor, are likely to beggar all of us. It is not impossible that our civilization will be wrecked by foolhardy individuals. Although one might listen to Cassandra, he need have no fear of the average man if he believed that parsimony were a more common trait than profusion. Capital would increase because people could improve their condition only by augmenting their fortunes.[22]

Even if the state were to cease interfering with the investment of private capital, the lack of foresight and good will of many a promoter would still cause bankruptcies. Nevertheless, the unsuccessful enterprises would be few in number, and the frugality and prudence of the majority could well afford to absorb them. Great nations have nothing to fear from the misfortunes of private individuals, but private individuals have much to fear from the misfortunes of great nations. An autocratic government has frequently been able to ruin a wealthy country, not so much by its unwarranted prodigality as by its foolish economic policies. A powerful oligarchy which desires to spend more than its income does not hesitate to encroach upon the capital of the country and thereby to undermine the entire economic structure; the funds which have formerly supported productive laborers are so seriously impaired that soon the annual produce of the nation commences to decline. The idle have ruined the industrious. Rome could probably have supported the riotous living of its nobility, but it was in no position to prop the national economy once its capital structure was impaired.

The contention that the state must control the economic life of its citizens for their own sake is clearly a sham, because there is no reason why a population, if left to itself, would undermine the prosperity of a country. It has, however, not been unusual for a government to ruin a country in its desire to further the public welfare.

Adam Smith, like all social philosophers except anarchists, was more interested in the commonwealth than in the individual members of the commonwealth. He believed that increasing the individual's scope of action was the surest way of speeding the progress of the community. Unseen hands facilitated this transformation; the procedure was not, however, very mysterious; it depended only upon the establishment of perfect justice, perfect liberty, and perfect equality. Perfection is not within the realm of human attainment, and Smith realized that he was guilty of wishful thinking in advancing these desiderata. He doubtless hoped that a struggle for natural liberty would at least result in the death of unnatural restraint.[23]

Every man should have the right to determine for himself the ways in which he desires to employ his capital. Under prevailing institutions, monopolies are advantageous to special interests, and profits are the reward, not of exertion and good judgment, but of the kind actions of a paternalistic government. Not a little of the nation's capital is therefore badly invested, and although a favorite minority is very wealthy, the general public is far from prosperous.

The restraints upon the working class must be removed because no possible justification can exist for increasing the difficulties of man's earning his bread by his labor. The impediments placed by the state in the path of agriculture should likewise be removed. The landed interest will be adversely affected as long as industry receives special aid, for no capital will be invested in agriculture if artificially high profits can be obtained in industrial and commercial undertakings. But any attempt of the landlords to overcome their disabilities by legislation is fore-doomed to failure.

The privileges and the disabilities of the several groups in the community have impeded the progress of the country, which could again be quickened if the contending classes would agree upon an overhauling of the system. The most efficient procedure would be to remove the special advantages and disadvantages of the different sectors of the population. A small minority would probably lose much of its wealth and prestige by such a house cleaning, but it would not be long before even this very group were compensated. For instance, if monopolies went by the board, merchants would have to be satisfied in the immediate future with a lower rate of profit. The country, however, would benefit greatly by a dissolution of the large corporations; national prosperity would doubtless increase, and the commercial interests would certainly profit greatly.

Adam Smith did not preach the doctrine of economic freedom for its own sake; he was much too critical of fanatics to be guilty of any fanaticism himself. He believed that the state control of industry was inimical to the true interests of the public and therefore, as a reformer, was confronted with but two possible lines of action. He could either suggest improvements in the techniques of regulation, or else advocate a more radical alteration of society which would make regulation unnecessary. Smith decided on the second approach.

He did not attack blindly, for he did not believe all state interference to be bad; consistency, in terms of an abstract principle, did not appeal to him. He did not hesitate for a moment to suggest that the commonwealth should be responsible for the upkeep of the highways, because it might be dangerous to permit private individuals to control them. The importance of inland trade routes need hardly be emphasized, although the fallacious mercantilistic doctrine maintained that the wealth of the country could be increased only by foreign trade. The more numerous and varied aspects of domestic commerce clearly prove its preeminent significance for the economy as a whole.[24] The state, out of consideration for the public welfare, should therefore control the highways of the land,

and ought not to trust private individuals with this
vital business.[25]

The passage of ships and barges depends upon the
navigability of the canals, disrepair of which will
immediately put an end to water transportation.
Private individuals can therefore be trusted with the
upkeep of the conduits and the collection of tolls,
because any failure in the service will at once termi-
nate their income. Hence the state need not interfere
to protect the public.

The welfare and health of the people are greatly
influenced by lighting and water supplies; it is therefore unwise to leave such vital services in the control
of private individuals, because no one man or group of
men will be able or interested to subscribe the necessary amount of capital for the erection of efficient
plants. The government ought to undertake this
work, but the commune should always be held responsible. The cost of lighting the streets of a city
should be met by local taxes rather than by monies
from the national treasury. Inefficiency, waste, and
fraud doubtless occur in the management of municipalities, but it is distinctly improbable that the abuses
of local administration equal those of the national
government. Furthermore, the local population will
be much more interested in efficient service if it is
forced to meet the bills.

Although Smith greatly disliked state interference
with the investment of capital, he did suggest the
retention of the statute which regulated the interest
rate. He feared that if the law were repealed, spend-
thrifts and profligates would contract at inordinately

high rates with the result that large amounts of capital would find their way into the hands of unproductive projectors.[26]

The Scottish economist hoped that his reforms, if introduced, would lead to a reduction in the price of goods and an enhancement in the quality of workmanship. He believed that these beneficial results could most easily be obtained by increasing competition in economic life. Despite this general approach, Smith did not object to the interference of the state with certain economic forces and, in the case of labor, argued strongly in favor of such action. In his opinion, public interest could best be served by the education of the populace, and he proposed the use of public monies for this purpose.

Smith advocated one reform which must have appeared reactionary even to the people of his time. It concerned the judiciary. The economic relations between members of a society are in no small measure influenced by the prevailing code of law, for wherever there is great property, there is great inequality. The law alone permits the prince to live in peace among the paupers.[27] The acquisition of valuable and extensive property would be impossible without the prior guarantee that its ownership and use will be protected by the civil authority.

The judiciary is therefore one of the most important of social institutions, and any inefficiency in the administration of the law is likely to have serious consequences. In very early times the sovereign dispensed justice with not unsatisfactory returns, for the adjudication of disputes netted him large sums of money. Corruption soon became prevalent. The rich plaintiffs who were usually on intimate terms with the king invariably won their suits. With the development of the modern state, the administration of justice was put upon an independent basis. Judges became civil servants.

Adam Smith did not view this development with favor; he therefore suggested that judges should be paid by the litigants. This proposal looked at first glance anomalous, but upon consideration it appeared more reasonable. Under the existing system, even though the state remunerated the interpreters of the law, the administration of justice was not free. The costs of counsel and the incidental court fees were high; now certain advantages might have resulted from adding the salaries of the judges to the general expenses of a lawsuit. The judiciary in England was not industrious; in fact, the diligence of the judges was very slight: one of the surest means to improve the work of the magistrates would have been to recompense them for their actual rather than for their supposed labor. This was the reason for Adam Smith's unusual proposal.

Smith believed political economy to have a two-fold purpose: that of enriching the people and the sovereign.[28] He found no difficulty, because of the broadness of his general approach, in including in his economic treatise lengthy discussions on education, government, and law. Social institutions could obviously exert a pronounced influence upon the economic scene. Though certain of his contemporaries considered Smith the best informed man since Aristotle,[29] he was no devotee of learning for learning's sake. In his native country the cultivation of the humanities for the ennoblement of the individual would have been scorned as unchristian and immoral. Hume's difficulties with the public resulted largely from his belief that the world was a stage upon which the actor had the right to perform for his own rather than for his audience's amusement. Smith, though he had genuine appreciation for Hume's intellectual powers, rather resented his friend's scepticism. The Scottish philosopher was intrigued by the thoughts of men; the Scottish economist was fascinated by the actions of men. When the latter published his treatise on economics, his early manifested predilection for the practical was more clearly accentuated. The complete title read: *An Inquiry into the Nature and Causes of the Wealth of Nations*, and might have continued with the subheading: *For the Purpose of Increasing the Same*.

It was in Kirkcaldy, where he had settled after his return from abroad, that Smith wrote the larger part of his book on political economy. When he left this town and set out for London in 1772, his friends assumed that his manuscript was complete, but to their great surprise the book did not see the light of day until four years later. Smith spent the intervening period in revising his work. He must have realized shortly after his arrival in London that his prolonged isolation in the small Scottish town was a mistake, in that he had failed to keep well informed on many contemporary problems. The sixties and seventies were important decades in English political history, and Smith did not hesitate to scrap a substantial part of his work when he discovered that events had made much of his analysis academic. Although the absent-minded professor once made tea of bread and butter and then declared it to be the worst beverage he ever drank, he never forgot the real world for any length of time. Another story declares that when Smith conducted Lord Townshend through Glasgow, he was so preoccupied with his own reflections that he walked into a tan pit. It was surely no ordinary Professor of Moral Philosophy who considered a tannery a show place for a lord.[30] Life interested this man.

Smith studied the nature and causes of wealth because he assumed that his researches would enable him more easily to attain his principal objective, that of increasing the prosperity of his own and other countries. Once the weak pivots in the existing social mechanism were discovered and repaired, the machine would function more smoothly. His treatise purports to outline the means to this end. But Smith was not solely interested in the creation of additional commodities. He realized that there would be little purpose in augmenting the products of industry unless more people could subsist in a better way.[31] Education played an important rôle in the Smithian analysis because it afforded one of the principal instrumentalities for reform; if the people knew how to read, they could learn to shun evil and seek virtue.

The keynote of Adam Smith's program was the extension of freedom in economic activities, but at no time did he become a worshiper of his own fetish. The benefits which were to accrue to the public through the introduction of the new techniques were always to be weighed against the disadvantages deriving from the new approach. This pragmatic attitude was at times obscured, because the master stylist occasionally wrote very floridly. The devil had to be painted in deep black in order to impress the ignorant with the true glory of God. Smith wrote in caressing terms about laissez faire because he was out to attack and if possible demolish the system of restraints which were choking English economic life. A few individuals had a strangle hold on the body corporate and Smith demanded in the name of the public that they release their grip. Timid souls had become so used to oppression that they feared the freedom which they did not possess.[32] To reassure these people, Smith drew a colorful picture of the future, though it is extremely doubtful whether he had much faith in his own art except as propaganda.[33]

The nineteenth-century writers, however, did not bother to discount Smith's work, for they felt certain that he had developed a coherent laissez faire philosophy. Did he not suggest that churches should compete with one another; that judges ought to be paid only for the work they perform; and that a colonial empire which proves costly ought to be sacrificed? Clearly, these interpreters could quote page after page to substantiate their analysis. On the other hand, they must have been slightly bothered by Smith's advocacy of state interference with education, highways, interest rates, specific industries and the like. The casual student, however, would have been justified in assuming that these formed minor deviations from a general thesis. The Scottish economist must have favored freedom, for it was the religion of the educated man of his day. One of his contemporaries even went so far as to remark that they were living in an "Age of Freedom."[34]

Subtler writers, however, carefully analyzed Adam Smith's preconceptions before they ventured to pass a verdict upon his work. One very able interpreter, Thorstein Veblen, believed that the most significant characteristic of the author of the *Wealth of Nations* was his animistic approach to his study of natural law and nature. Newtonian physics was held in awe by the eighteenth-century intellectuals, especially by those who were not scientists. The harmonious working of a machine of many parts fascinated these people, and hence they were constantly applying the analysis of Sir Isaac to non-mechanical problems. Many considered man himself to be a machine.[35] It is not surprising, therefore, that Smith has been accused of transplanting Newtonian mechanics into economics, substituting in the process laissez faire for the law of gravitation.[36] But this is truly doubtful. Smith was probably talking in common parlance, in the language which he had learnt at home and in school. But the same terms can be used for entirely different purposes. People of diametrically opposed points of view were constantly appealing to the law of nature and of nations;[37] in fact, they had been doing so for centuries.[38] But if the devil quotes Scripture, there is no reason to confuse him with the saints because they do likewise.

An attempt has also been made to explain Smith's work as a rationalization for the changes in eighteenth-

century society. The merchants and the manufacturers
in the new commercial and industrial centers of
England and Scotland were anxious to put an end to
the existing system of governmental restraints which
they discovered were costing them a pretty penny.
Adam Smith supposedly obliged them by working out
in a methodical fashion—he was a university professor—a defense for their attitude.[39] The evidence to
the contrary, however, is not easily dismissed. One
of the leading men in Scotland wrote to Smith after
the publication of the *Wealth of Nations* that his
book had managed so far to "provoke the church,
the universities, the merchants—and likewise the
militia."[40] An exponent of popular prejudices seldom
antagonizes many classes and individuals. A careful
reading of Smith's attacks upon the princes of trade
would hardly leave one reason to believe that he was
their attorney; nor does the least evidence exist that
he ever committed himself to plead their case.

The spirit molds the flesh. Historical analysis
must attempt to recapture the emotional characteristics of the subject under investigation; all else is
secondary. The many pages devoted to the prices of
wheat and silver in the *Wealth of Nations* are most
unimportant, for they shed very little light upon the
author; but the many paragraphs which extol the
agricultural and the laboring classes do offer very
significant clues. Adam Smith devoted his genius and
his energies to enhancing the social and economic
status of the community, and these two groups
combined, represented by far the larger sector of the
population. In his opinion a strong minority had

successfully feathered its nest at the expense of farmers and laborers. Hence the nation at large had suffered. Laissez faire can be a powerful weapon in the class struggle; it can deprive the wealthy of their illegitimate gains. Smith's treatise is weighed down by much extraneous material; it is not easy fully to appreciate the focus of the attack. But fortunately we possess a lengthy dissertation by Smith on a non-economic problem in which his laissez faire approach is clearly delineated. This time he was not writing for publication and therefore his remarks are likely to be an even truer reflection of his intimate beliefs.

The Duke of Buccleugh, his old pupil, wrote to him requesting his views on a proposal then before Parliament to investigate the lax practices of Scottish universities in granting medical degrees. Smith introduces his reply by stating that he would favor an investigation if the matter appeared to be of great public concern but, on the other hand, it would be foolish for the government to meddle in the affairs of a body corporate if the issues raised were only of slight interest to the community.[41] One of the proposed reforms would prohibit any student from being admitted to final examinations for the degree unless he could prove attendance at the university for at least two years. Smith believes this to be a foolish regulation, and very oppressive upon private teachers. Assuredly, the students of Hunter and Hewson, who are taught privately, are as well trained as any university graduate. To enforce two years academic training upon all future members of the medical profession would result in establishing a monopoly in favor of the colleges. Now monopolies are usually dangerous, and the service which they render is seldom of high quality because they are always assured of a market for their product. Smith is firmly convinced that the public would suffer through the establishment of this new regulation.

The universities of Europe and especially those of England have fallen into a state of degradation and contempt. The professors are not held to account for their work, and they receive their salaries irrespective of the quality of their instruction. The present autocracy of the colleges is alarming but not critical; however, there are reasons to suspect that their monopolistic privileges will be increased after a parliamentary visitation. Smith is the last to deny the inadequacy of the existing system, but he fears that the projected reforms will make matters worse. No one, of course can defend the practice of signing a student's diploma because he is well known to the bursar, though almost a total stranger to the faculty. Most colleges are primarily interested in forcing a student to spend a great deal of money during the course of his residence, and one who has complied with the fiscal regulations of the university is seldom failed in his examinations.

The degree is obviously no guarantee of the candidate's good sense and discretion, but testifies only that he has memorized the prescribed number of formulae and read the required texts. If the medical diploma is nothing but a scrap of paper, it should be recognized as such by the public, for then simple people would no longer be exploited.

The older universities graduate their medical pupils only after eleven or more years' residence; the poorer colleges in order to draw students to their campuses have therefore commenced to sell degrees. This is doubtless an infamous practice but it has had two enviable results. In the first place, if this competition did not take place, few people in England could afford to pay the price of having their pulse taken. A doctor's worth in the second place is no longer determined by his membership in an exclusive corporation, but depends entirely upon his own ability; he can no longer fleece the public because he has spent a decade doing nothing at Oxford or Cambridge. The physicians who have devoted long years to securing their diplomas are probably not overfond of their many competitors who have purchased theirs after a very short college career. Smith is convinced that those members of the profession who fear the breakdown of their monopolistic privileges are responsible for advocating the investigation of the Scottish medical schools. However, he advises against the visitation because he views with favor the increase in the number of free-lance physicians. The price of medical service can be reduced and the public benefited only through the destruction of the existing monopoly.

Smith concludes his epistle with the remark that he will probably get his lug (ear) in his lufe (hand) for what he has written, but having been asked for his opinion he could do no less than give it. He is not overjoyed with his own conclusions, for clearly his advice against the visitation is tacit approval of the existing system of roguery and sham. It is exceedingly difficult for a former professor of Christian ethics to defend these depraved conditions, but Smith has the courage of his convictions. He prefers to flirt with the devil rather than to worship false gods. He is first and foremost concerned with the public welfare and all his judgments on matters of social policy are determined with reference to this one criterion. Smith is fully aware that the public suffers distinct hurt from the prevailing immoral practice which enables students to buy their doctor's diplomas, but he is by no means convinced that governmental interference could remedy the situation. In fact, he is certain that if the state commenced to meddle it could only succeed in making bad worse.

Perhaps laissez faire will still make this a better world for all.

Part Two

False Prophets

In the past, history has concerned itself with the military exploits of distinguished brigands; today history concerns itself with the amatory exploits of psychopathic personalities. No one can foresee the history of tomorrow. But in all ages, history has been an exercise in the study of values. Campo Formio, Moscow, Leipzig are starred in the old textbooks; Josephine, Maria Louisa, Countess Walewski share the honors in the new ones. Yet the mystery of how the stout little Corsican, who was weaned by his mother, spanked by his father, and educated by his priest, gained the throne of France is still unsolved. History remains an eternal mystery.

Adam Smith was the patron saint of nineteenth-century capitalism, but his contemporaries did not even consider him a holy man. He distinctly aroused the animosity of the best people in 1776, but some years later he was loudly applauded by their children. The younger set enjoyed much freedom; they were therefore favorably inclined toward the prophet of laissez faire. People like to have their prejudices and practices find favor; they become most disagreeable when their pet beliefs are attacked. Now, there can be no doubt that Adam Smith was one of those unpleasant individuals who scorned the confirmed opinions of his contemporaries and strove to alter them. Smith was primarily concerned with mercantilism; the nineteenth century believed that his major interest centered in a defense of capitalism. This latter point of view is however completely untenable. During the lifetime of Adam Smith, the modern industrial organization was not yet born; true, England was pregnant, a delivery was expected, but the sex of the child was unknown.[1]

To consider Adam Smith an economist of capitalism is not only misleading, it is wrong—unless one applies the term capitalism, as many writers have done, to the economic order which developed in western Europe after the decline of feudalism. One can use the word thus; it then becomes important to point out that Smith was not an economist of modern industrialism. This is not futile quibbling. The contributions of Adam Smith to modern thought cannot possibly be appreciated unless one realizes that he lived and labored in a pre-machine civilization.

Economics is not theology, and its theories are not *sub specie æternitatis*. A most intimate relation must exist between the doctrines expounded by an economist and the institutions of the economist's civilization. A theory of irredeemable currency would not be developed in a community which transacted all of its sales in metallic money. To appreciate the ideological development of Adam Smith, careful consideration must be paid to the structure of industry in his day; though his thoughts were not determined they were surely influenced by his environment. Unless one reconstructs the economic organization which the

Wealth of Nations presupposes, one will not be able to evaluate correctly the author's theories.

During the century and a half which separated the reigns of the Virgin Queen and George the Third, England had undergone not a few changes. The population and wealth of the country had increased, a colonial empire had been firmly established, the power of the crown had decreased, the nobility had been forced to pay some respect to the new bourgeoisie, the Established Church had witnessed the mutiplication of the dissenters . . . and yet, despite all these changes, England was still England. The improvement in agriculture had lessened the price of food products, dwellings had become more habitable, and the number of ditches had decreased; but people ate much the same food, lived in much the same houses, and traveled in much the same way as they had in previous generations.

England under Elizabeth was not very peaceful, for a revolution was on foot. The merchants, freed of the shackles of medieval restraint, were reorganizing the national economy. Modern business enterprise was born. Despite the energy and assiduity of the commercial class, the nation's wealth grew slowly, for the niggardliness of nature impeded the rapidity of economic progress. The struggle with the soil which engaged the largest number of people was hard and unremunerative.

At the time when Adam Smith published the *Wealth of Nations* the inhabitants of England worked the land, engaged in manufacturing, or plied trades.

Naturally, the country had changed since the days of the illustrious queen, but the developments which had occurred were not startling. For instance, Glasgow had been an unimportant community in the years following the Reformation, and it was only during Adam Smith's lifetime that the city commenced to expand.[2] The leather, copper and shoe industries were not founded before the middle of century; in 1767 only eight pounds in tonnage fees were collected, and sometimes for weeks on end no ship was seen on the water.[3] Not many years later, this Scottish river town became the most important commercial and industrial center in the British Isles, London alone excepted.

The Elizabethan merchant sought profits and the Victorian banker was motivated by the same desire, but the economic milieu of these two money jugglers were vastly different. The introduction of power machinery just before Adam Smith's death changed the entire landscape of England.

The dating of the power revolution is of fundamental importance in the evaluation of the *Wealth of Nations,* for an economic theory of industrialism will differ greatly from an economic theory of a handicraft civilization. Adam Smith himself solves the problem of chronology. He relates that one man frequently found it feasible to supervise his entire working staff, a condition which could only have existed when factories were operated on a small scale. Furthermore, we read in the *Wealth of Nations* that a pin-manufacturing plant despite the minute subdivision of the productive process frequently did not house more than ten laborers. In the eighteenth century

machinery was unimportant except in the heavy industries; one was considered a great industrialist if
he employed a thousand pounds annually in the
support of his fixed capital.[4] Most people expended
very little money on industrial equipment: the tailor,
the shoemaker and the clothier were primarily
interested in the price of labor and materials.[5]

In Smith's day stockings knit by hand undersold
those produced on a loom.[6] Hand labor can never
compete successfully with machine labor unless the
mechanical apparatus is very imperfect; for no matter
how greatly the artisan reduces his standard of living,
he cannot match the machine's low cost of upkeep.
Smith was therefore probably justified in not being
impressed by the rate of technological improvement
in his own and the preceding centuries. It is true that a
marked advance in the manufacture of metal products
must have taken place, because the price of a watch
dropped within a hundred years from twenty pounds
to twenty shillings; and in general the commodities
produced at Birmingham and Sheffield became much
cheaper.[7] On the other hand, the important clothing
industry did not show any evidence of technical advance; the price of cloaks and suits had not been
reduced for decades and there was even reason to sur-
mise that the better quality wearing apparel had of
late become more expensive. In order to discern an
improvement in this branch of manufacturing, one
would have been forced to compare conditions in the
eighteenth century with those in the fifteenth.[8]

The comparative stability of English industrial
society during the lifetime of Smith can be further

judged by the fact that he chose agriculture as a
typical example of a dynamic enterprise; he pointed
out that while spinners and weavers produce approximately the same quantity of linen and woolen
goods every year, the efficiency of farm hands varies
greatly. This sentence must have been written before
modern technology had made any marked inroads
into the economic structure, because after the birth of
machinery agriculture proved to be more static than
manufacturing.

Modern industrialism would have been impossible
without power, and power would have been impossible without coal. England, although she had the
exceptional good fortune to possess a most ample
coal supply, waited many years before she commenced
to exploit her deposits. It is true that coal had been
mined long before Adam Smith was born, but in no
great quantities. Extraction was difficult and transportation costly. At first it was shipped only within small
areas; Shropshire and Newcastle coal could not compete.[9] Manufacturers built their plants in the immediate vicinity of the mines because the benefits
which they derived from the use of coal would have
been dissipated had they been forced to pay the costs
of extended transportation.[10] Throughout the eighteenth century Parliament was very considerate of the
welfare of the merchant and the manufacturer; however, it evidenced no interest in the coal trade. Adam
Smith considered this indifference most unfortunate
and therefore exerted himself to effect a change in the
attitude of the legislature. He was even willing,
despite his abhorrence of bounties, to indorse a

subsidy upon the transportation of coal, because he believed that its more widespread consumption would lead to beneficial results. The foolish government instead of aiding its transport placed a tax of 60 percent on all coal shipped coastwise. Clearly, the manufacturers must have been comparatively indifferent to the price of coal, for otherwise they doubtless could have had the levy reduced or repealed.[11]

In Adam Smith's day wood was still frequently used for fuel. Furthermore, industry had not yet shifted in any large degree to the mining district of Newcastle.[12] Inasmuch as the important changes in the economic structure of the country did not take place until coal came into common use, the Industrial Revolution must have taken place after the publication of the *Wealth of Nations*.

It is extremely doubtful whether the writings of any man have ever materially affected the course of human events; books can never possess the same potency as economic and social forces. However, the letters on a printed page are not infrequently transformed into living institutions. The metamorphosis is often not clear to the observer; what he assumes to be a direct cause-and-effect sequence is frequently nothing else than the fortuitous fulfillment of a wishful hypothesis.

Critics have maintained that the *Wealth of Nations* exerted the most pronounced influence upon British governmental policies. The book upon its appearance in 1776 sold well, though the journals did not favor it with extended reviews. Probably, the *Theory of Moral Sentiments* had whetted the taste of many for

the work of Adam Smith.[13] However, in 1780 Smith
in ordering several copies of the *Wealth of Nations*
remarked that he had almost forgotten that he had
written it; he added facetiously that he was probably
the only customer for his book. Smith was doubtless
overmodest, for a second edition had already appeared and three more were to be published before his
death. The book had been translated into French,
German and Italian. Hence the author's dissatisfaction
cannot be understood unless one considers that much-
desired recognition from Parliamentary leaders was
not forthcoming.[14] The statesmen who controlled the
economic and political policies of Great Britain had,
with very few exceptions, ignored the book. Fox,
perhaps the most powerful man in Parliament, ridiculed it and even went so far as to consider the Earl
of Lauderdale's admiration for the *Wealth of Nations*
an unfortunate aberration of an otherwise healthy
mind.[15]

Smith did succeed in influencing one of England's
foremost statesmen, though not so much by his
writing as by his conversation. He once journeyed
with Lord Shelbourne from Glasgow to London and
during the trip discoursed at length upon his economic
theories. The future prime minister learned to appreciate the beauties of Smith's doctrines; they became for
him a cause of abiding joy. But the Scottish reformer
was not often so successful.[16] Despite the fact that
Parliament constantly debated economic and social
issues, the *Wealth of Nations*, until eight years after
publication, was not quoted by any member. It would
have been natural for one of the speakers to refer to

this work but its prestige was obviously not sufficient to warrant the legislator's regard.

England was not at all ruffled by the publication of Adam Smith's book; the country did not suddenly cease its evil ways and commerce to practice virtue. Those who read the *Wealth of Nations* were for the most part impressed by the author's shrewd analysis and reasonable suggestions. But kings were not philosophers nor philosophers kings, and the Scottish economist was unable to affect the country's policies. Some twenty-five or fifty years later, however, the hopes and aspirations of Adam Smith were largely realized, and even his extravagant dream about free trade had come true. One can well understand, therefore, why Buckle maintained that the *Wealth of Nations* was the most important book ever written, a book which had done more to advance human welfare than any other single document. The nineteenth-century British essayist greatly admired the civilization of his day; he believed it to represent the highest development of man's creative genius. In his opinion, Adam Smith had contributed greatly to this progress by first haranguing the multitude on the beauties of the new utopia. Buckle's laudation of Smith was likely exaggerated; perhaps it was entirely unjustifiable. A review of the evidence can alone decide the issue.

Prior to 1789 the British had encouraged the incendiary activities of the French radicals, but thereafter their attitude changed, for they discovered that the flames might spread across the Channel. Louis XVI and Marie Antoinette had been beheaded. Fear and trepidation broke out in England. The leaders of British culture introduced the most reactionary policies in order to insure that London should never witness a similar spectacle. They commenced their work as soon as they became aware that the French agitators were more interested in an efficient than in a glorious revolution.[17]

All liberals were placed under suspicion and all reform movements were outlawed. It was known that Adam Smith had been intimately acquainted with the leaders of the French Enlightenment; furthermore, he had consistently attacked intrenched privileges. Hence during the violent period of reaction, Adam Smith went into eclipse; in fact, political economy became taboo; fear and anxiety reigned supreme.[18]

Toward the end of the eighteenth century the British Isles were in a state of great upheaval, even though English political life was remarkably stable. Changes were occurring on the economic front. The power machine disturbed England quite as much as Danton's demagoguery excited France. The older system of production and exchange commenced to disintegrate with marked rapidity, and many institutions of the old domestic economy were becoming rapidly anachronistic. The apprenticeship and settlement statutes which had so disturbed Adam Smith were permitted to lapse, once the new factories created a demand for workers.[19] The state stood by, while the rebellion against its authority gained momentum.

Smith had directed his attack against mercantilism —against the special favors which the commercial classes had managed to obtain for themselves in the form of bounties, drawbacks, subsidies, monopolies, and the like. Had he lived to the age of a hundred he would have witnessed the unbelievable; the merchant princes and the master manufacturers were no longer interested in the continuation of their many privileges, and not a small number of the new bourgeoisie were distinctly antagonistic to state paternalism.[20] In Smith's day England's trade with the Far East, Africa and America was considered of vital importance, and the several joint-stock and regulated companies which engaged in commerce with these distant parts were carefully protected and encouraged. Indians, Negroes, and Colonials became much less important after the power machine greatly enhanced the productivity of English industry; the European market could doubtless absorb many more British wares than the barbarians the world over. In order to exploit the newly discovered El Dorados, both at home and abroad, the industrialists, believing that a good-natured but meddling government was more of a hindrance than a help, attempted to free themselves from all state interference.

Adam Smith had of course argued for the cessation of governmental interference in business, a policy which was now, at the beginning of the nineteenth century, to be adopted. The divorce, however, was not due to his expert pleading, but rather to the influence of the power machine. It can hardly be argued that Smith was conscious of the growing dominance of the Frankenstein monster when one remembers the insignificant rôle which the mechanical arts played in his analysis.

Smith probably did not change his basic approach
to economics from the time when he first lectured to
his extension class in Edinburgh. The major technological improvements in industry were for the most
part introduced after 1770;[21] it would therefore have
been impossible for his economic theories to have reflected the incidence of machine production. The
focus of Smith's attack was entirely different. He
believed that the existing economic organization with
its many privileges and restraints was impeding the
nation's progress; more especially he objected to the
exploitation of the farming and the laboring groups
by the shrewd mercantile class. Smith therefore set
himself the task of undertaking an analysis which he
hoped would eventually lead to reforms. The *Wealth
of Nations* can only be appreciated against this background. Now, the book does present a beautiful
synthetic study of eighteenth-century England with
the author's critical comments and emendations. It is
clearly not an apology for the prevailing economic
organization for, if so it would have gone the way of
all apologies. Nor did the book survive because of its
caustic attack on mercantilism. If Adam Smith had
never written one sentence, mercantilism would have
died and England would have become a great industrial country. The author's reputation and his
admirable literary style probably saved the book from
immediate oblivion. But its later fame was in no
way associated with its intrinsic qualities. The story
of this most interesting paradox in the history of
thought has yet to be told.

Smith taught economics at Edinburgh and Glasgow for fifteen years, and after retiring from academic life continued to engage in economic research for an additional quarter of a century. Moreover, his interest in the subject did not end with the publication of his magnum opus; several years thereafter he added to the original text eighty pages of new material.[22] Smith, though he lived sixty years and more, failed to attract any brilliant students; what little personal influence he exercised was upon his associates, Hume and Ferguson. He founded no school, for a school without pupils is a contradiction in terms; nor was he, as some historians assume, the founder of the science of economics.

Although many books and pamphlets in the field of economics were written in the years immediately following the publication of the *Wealth of Nations*, not one work of major importance appeared until 1798 when Malthus presented the world with his *Essay on Population*. Systematic treatises on economics did not appear until the second and third decades of the nineteenth century: Ricardo's *Principles of Political Economy and Taxation* was published in 1817; Malthus' *Political Economy* in 1820; Mill's *Elements of Political Economy* in the following year.

These three authors had never studied under Smith, but they nevertheless considered themselves his pupils; it mattered little that they were stimulated by his books rather than by his lectures. Thomas Malthus stated that the *Wealth of Nations* was partly responsible for arousing his interest in the problem of population.[23] David Ricardo is reputed to have been completely ignorant of the science of economics until he chanced to read the *Wealth of Nations*. Clearly these men must have felt deeply indebted to Smith.[24] John Stuart Mill, the acknowledged successor of the older classical economists, was considered for many decades the outstanding representative of scientific economics. In the introduction to his *Principles of Political Economy*, the younger Mill remarkes that he plans to imitate Adam Smith and write a *Wealth of Nations* for the nineteenth century.[25] Karl Marx, one of the best historians of political economy, took occasion to point out that Mill's boast reminds him of a drunken sergeant who imagines himself to be Wellington.[26] Unfortunately, Marx's sarcasm was not totally unwarranted, for the nineteenth century economists had no legitimate ground to consider themselves the lineal descendants of the distinguished Scottish economist.

Ricardo's family tree was established by later investigators, and he himself never put forward any claims to relationship.[27] The retired stockbroker did, however, refer to Smith on many occasions. In the original preface to the first edition of the *Principles*, Ricardo acknowledges the contributions of Smith, Turgot, Steuart, Say, and Sismondi, though he regretfully reflects upon the fact that these men had failed to study the natural course of rent, profit and wages. To place Smith in the company of Turgot and Sismondi is pardonable, but to group him with Steuart and Say is a major crime, for Steuart was an uninspired defender of mercantilism, and Say a mediocre vulgarizer of Smith.[28]

David Ricardo was a modest man who felt very keenly, especially during the years when he engaged in economic research, the lack of a formal education. He even hesitated to publish his reflections upon political economy and probably would never have done so had it not been for the continuous coaxing of his friends. His failure to appreciate Adam Smith was very probably the result of his insufficient cultural training. Ricardo despite the fact that he was in fundamental disagreement with Smith, did not hesitate to quote him for illustrative or corroborative purposes. He believed that economics should be primarily concerned with an analysis of distribution in a static state; Smith was interested in production in a dynamic society.[29] The *Principles* is therefore full of intricate and delicate analyses of many and difficult problems, but the historical, sociological, and political discussions which fill the *Wealth of Nations* are missing. Ricardo devotes an entire chapter to a consideration of Malthus's theory of rent, though he finds no occasion to discuss law, education, and the church. Economics, having been put on a diet, has lost not a little weight. Ricardo was fascinated by the forces which established profits at the prevailing rate, wages at a subsistence level, and rents on all except marginal land. He could juggle profits, wages, and rent in much the same way as a mathematician could play with integers.

The classical economists were not indifferent to the real world; they set out deliberately to discover the laws of business enterprise. They made one basic assumption, namely, that economic theory could aid in the solution of practical difficulties. There existed in the society of their day an antagonism between the property owners and the laborers, and the economists were led to study in some detail the relation of wages to profits. They developed long and learned arguments to prove that wages and profits vary inversely. This law was a truism and hence could not be demolished by logical arguments. Although the public is seldom interested in truisms or logic, it is always concerned with food and clothing. It happened that the scholarly gentlemen in developing their scientific analysis obscured the one important consideration, that an increase in productivity would enable both owner and worker to receive a larger amount of real income.

The classical economists not only were oblivious to the shortcomings of their analyses, but believed them to possess the greatest significance. The discovery of the law of profits and wages made them prophets by enabling them to forecast the future; clearly the inverse relation between these two factors would never change.

Adam Smith, however, had few rigid elements in his theoretic structure, and these he confined to the realm of human conduct where he believed one might presuppose a minimum of stability. For instance, the legislator must always be governed by the same general principles because he cannot afford to sacrifice honor, justice, and decency for a momentary advantage. Only a cheap politician follows an opportunistic approach.[30]

Adam Smith, because of his primary interest in the development of institutions, made few static assumptions in his very dynamic treatise on economics. The *Wealth of Nations* is directed toward changing the prevailing economic structure. Production would be enhanced by a removal of the mercantilistic restrictions on industry; the productivity of labor would be increased by the widespread introduction of primary education; profits would be lowered by forcing Parliament to cease meddling in business. Smith believed the world to be imperfect; he devoted his energies to improving it. He did not care to discover why profits were 15 and not 10 percent; he was most anxious to discover a means of decreasing the prevailing rate, because he believed that such action would benefit the public. Science for science's sake was not an eighteenth century ideal, and even Hume was more moralist than skeptic. The classical economists, however, accepted the institutions of their day and devoted their talents to analysing the social mechanism. Adam Smith of course had certain postulates. He did not question private property, although he made various invidious remarks as to its origin. He furthermore assumed that the state was responsible for the preservation of order. In addition, he thought that the family offered the best means of regulating the relation of the sexes. Despite these and other theses, there remained a very wide range of questions which the Scottish economist investigated upon an empirical rather than a logical basis.

The classical writers were primarily interested in the manipulation of concepts; they were most anxious to determine the range of variability of rent, wages, and profits. These men were all dominated by an in-

stinct for workmanship, for their ideal of intellectual
efficiency consisted in the development of finespun
logical analyses. Whether they realized the implications of their own procedure is extremely doubtful.
They were, one and all, under the influence of Jeremy
Bentham, and hence were vitally concerned with the
reform of British society through legislative action.[31]
Their treatises, however, did not show the influence
of their practical activities. These economists were
split personalities.

An unconscious admiration for the industrial system and a lack of historical perspective greatly influenced the work of the classical school. Although
the industrial civilization was very young, in fact just
coming out of its swaddling clothes, these writers
wrote as if it had existed from the first day of creation
and was likely to survive until the end of the world.

Malthus was greatly disturbed to discover one
morning that if the current trend in population were to
continue for any length of time, the food supply of the
country would prove insufficient and hence a large
number of people would die of starvation. No one
could possibly doubt the truth of this contention if he
would consider that increases in the productive quality
of the land could in no way keep pace with the productive powers of man. Malthus was much concerned
with the welfare of the poor and therefore implored
them for their own good to forego early marriages and
practice martial restraint; otherwise they could not
possibly escape their doom. In order to lend weight to
his arguments, Malthus outlined the ravages of famine
in past ages; he failed to report that rich people had

never died of hunger.[32] The Episcopal minister was not willing to admit that a causal relation could possibly exist between the distribution of wealth, and the welfare of the laboring class; in fact, he proved by logical analysis that even in a communistic state men, would die of starvation if they multiplied too rapidly.

The population of England had grown from a few thousands to millions but the country had never been seriously threatened by famine. Why did Malthus suddenly become panicky and deny that things could continue as they had been in the past? His uneasiness probably resulted from his unconscious realization that an increase in population would lead to important changes in society.[33] He therefore failed to consider that the productivity of man would doubtless influence the productivity of the land. There had been improvements in agricultural techniques in the past; there would be improvements in agricultural techniques in the future. Malthus directed his attack against those very people who advocated the reorganization of society; he felt quite certain that his law of population would put an end to all this talk about the perfectability of mankind. It is not inconceivable that in the reformed state Episcopal ministers might find themselves without benefices, a prospect which Thomas Malthus could hardly view with equanimity. He was in fact a typical sufferer from a fear psychosis, a disease all too common in England after the French Revolution.

Malthus's deductions were obtained from the study of a world which, for purposes of analysis, was intentionally arrested. His conclusions, however, were

pertinent only in a dynamic society. It was clearly unwarranted to assume that because man was increasing
very rapidly (a dynamic concept) many people were
certain at some later date to starve to death. The institutional structure would undergo many changes
before the population would press too greatly on the
food supply, but Malthus's abhorrence of reforms prevented him from realizing their inevitability.

Ricardo's analysis likewise suffered from a confusion of statics and dynamics. He assumed in the *Principles* that man in order to obtain sufficient food would
be forced to have recourse to ever-poorer lands, with
the result that rents would rise interminably. He forgot, however, as did Malthus and many others, that
man is never completely passive.[34]

The classical economists made the great mistake of
undertaking investigations at a specific time, within a
specific cultural scheme, and projecting their results
until they became independent of both time and place.
This approach enabled them to disregard the prospects
of institutional change and hence to avoid the moral-
istic implications of Scottish economics.

Adam Smith considered his society neither natural
nor normal and therefore anxiously looked forward to
the time when conditions would be changed. Normality existed only in the author's mind, but he hoped
that his reforms would introduce it to a small degree in
the real world. The *natural* and the *normal* were idealized concepts for Adam Smith. During the decades
following the publication of the *Wealth of Nations*,
England's industrial structure underwent radical trans-
formations, and at the time when the classical econo-

mists commenced to write, many of Smith's aspirations had been realized at least in form if not in spirit. For this reason Ricardo's *normal laws*, despite their abstract formulation, were actually closer to reality than Smith's analyses of normality.[35] Ricardo was interested in the present; Smith idealized the future.

Society can be studied from two standpoints: either the past can be reviewed for the purpose of explaining the present, or else the present can be analyzed in the hope of conjecturing the future. History cannot be studied without a point of view, and the historian can never strip himself of emotional bias.[36] Adam Smith devoted a substantial part of the *Wealth of Nations* to a review of the social, economic, and intellectual development of England from the decline of feudalism until the eighteenth century. Furthermore, he analyzed the society of his day in the light of his program of reform. The classical economists were interested neither in the past nor in the future; their entire energies were devoted to a study of the business economy of their own day. Despite Smith's disapproval of political arithmetic, Ricardo and his colleagues made economics a mathematical science; their equations were equations of production, consumption, exchange and distribution.

John Stuart Mill believed that Ricardo had solved certain technical problems for all time. He assumed for instance that the theory of value which the former stockbroker had developed could never be improved; it was perfect.[37] The man who set out to become the Adam Smith of the nineteenth century was, however, closer to the spirit of his idol than most economists.

Mill did entertain the prospect of altering certain social institutions, for he believed that the distribution of income could be changed.[38] On the other hand, he could not contemplate any interference with the *natural* laws of production. Mill was willing to admit that man could affect the distribution but not the production of wealth. Transcendentalism was, however, foreign to the eighteenth century, and assuredly foreign to Adam Smith.

Although the nineteenth-century economists believed that they were preaching the gospel of the Scottish sage, their writings denied those of their master. They were false prophets.

Hell Called Heaven

Man is a vain animal; he feels contented only if admired and adored. Although he is rather stupid, he does realize that his success in improving this world has not been very great. This knowledge interferes with his ego worship. Language offers him an excellent opportunity to compensate, for black can be called white; dirtiness, cleanliness; vice, virtue. It is much easier to live a contented existence in a fool's paradise than in a realist's hell.

The sons of Adam in expiation for their father's original sin have been forced to live in an unstable world, and their punishment will not cease until the coming of the Messiah. Man, though he principally desires security, has been forced to accept transience; being something of a coward, he meets the dilemma by dreaming of Elysium while traveling between Scylla and Charybdis.

Toward the end of the eighteenth century England was suddenly forced to alter her way of life. For a very long time conditions had been peaceful; a revolution had been so slow in coming that the king did not even lose his head when it finally arrived. In 1720 the bursting of the South Sea Bubble had caused some slight disturbance, but the community was not unduly ruffled; it was rather difficult to upset the emotional tranquillity of a stolid people. Adam Smith was born

three years after the financial debacle; he died just as
England was preparing for a lengthy struggle with
revolutionary France. During his lifetime many events
of major and minor importance took place, but for the
most part these occurred in the far corners of the earth
—in India and America, not in England. Within the
confines of the land things had moved slowly: population had increased; urban centers had grown; agricultural techniques had been refined.

Smith passed his entire life, with the exception of
the two years that he spent abroad, in Kirkcaldy,
Edinburgh, Glasgow, Oxford, and London. He knew
these towns as a young man, and with the exception of
Oxford, revisited them in his declining years; but they
had not changed greatly during this half century.

David Ricardo was born shortly before the *Wealth
of Nations* was published and died in 1823. During his
fifty-one years many more startling events occurred
than in the longer life span of Adam Smith.

The production and distribution of goods have always absorbed the major effort of man, and he has
therefore, in the hope of easing his labors, experi-
mented with every possible material. Ever since fire
was discovered in pre-historic times, man has been
adding to his technical achievements; his progress has
been slow. It came to pass that during the lifetime of
Adam Smith the inventive faculties of man had a very
successful inning; hence in the following years things
commenced to happen.

The industrial cataclysm which swept over England in the closing years of the eighteenth and the
early years of the nineteenth century must have

disturbed not a few placid souls.[1] The power machine had wrenched itself free from its creator and having learnt to reproduce by self-fertilization had no difficulty in dodging all controls. The moorings with the past were being very rapidly severed, and men, ever fearful of the unknown, sought desperately to retain a few connections with their old established world; they were even willing to grasp at a straw. One bright individual suddenly threw them that straw. He recalled the learned Scottish economist who had foretold that the disruption of the national economy would in the end turn out for the best.

The casual reader of the *Wealth of Nations* and the *Principles of Political Economy and Taxation* is impressed with the formal similarity between these two works, for Ricardo constantly employs words, phrases, and concepts which were first used by Adam Smith. The informed reader will be slightly suspicious of these superficial similarities, for he will be impressed by the very marked difference in the fundamental structure of the two treatises.

In Adam Smith's time production was organized on a small scale; owner and worker frequently labored side by side. Fixed capital was comparatively unimportant, and the majority of the workers owned their tools. Frequently one could engage in both agriculture and manufacturing; the cottage laborer worked his farm at one season and his loom at another.

At the beginning of the nineteenth century things had changed, and within the next few years continued to do so even more rapidly; the points of contact with the past grew increasingly indistinct. The pecuniary and the industrial phases of modern capitalism became sharply differentiated, for manufacturers lost almost all interest in the productive process; money profits were now their major concern.[2] At this time the modern factory developed. The city slums expanded because the industrial establishments employed large numbers of people.[3] Cottage laborers were either forced to leave the land because of the inclosures, or else were enticed by high money wages to seek work in the cities.[4] In any case, the domestic laborers would soon have been forced to give up the ghost because they could not long have competed with the new machines. A large part of the working population found itself in congested cities without a single possession in the world except its labor power.

After the first flush of prosperity, many workers were unable to capitalize that single possession. The expensive machinery greatly simplified the productive process; both skill and brawn were of slight importance, and women and children, because they could be paid lower wages, were frequently employed while the male members of the household were without work.

Adam Smith had advanced a laissez faire philosophy because in the society of his day the intimate alliance between the merchant princes and the state proved itself a very efficient means of exploiting the public. He believed that injurious class legislation could be checked only if governmental control of industry could be abolished.[5] His doctrine was naturally severely attacked by the commercial classes, for they feared the loss of their intrenched privileges. With the development of the industrial system after Smith's death, business men ceased their obstructionist policies and became ardent advocates of Smithian economics. They probably discovered that the state was no longer enhancing their profits and perhaps was even impeding their progress. Sometimes a helping hand is much desired; at other times it is strongly resented. Industry had reached that stage in its development where governmental coddling was detrimental. Industry had become sufficient unto itself. The advocates of a laissez faire economy were certain to quote the arguments of the learned Scottish economist who had first suggested the cessation of state interference with business.

Time obscures purposes; man even forgot that he was not made for the Sabbath, but that the Sabbath was made for him. Now within as short a period as twenty-five years, English writers had become completely oblivious to the motivation of Adam Smith in propounding his thesis of freedom. He had most assuredly not been interested in extending any favors to the merchants and the manufacturers, but had rather attempted to discover a means of rescuing the public from the clutches of these rapacious animals. Smith was primarily concerned with the public welfare, and so for that matter, were the classical economists. But there was a difference between the two. The latter, though they believed that a policy of non-interference would lead to beneficial results demanded the establishment of this system on the ground that it alone secured Englishmen their inviolable rights. Smith had used a similar argument in order to support his case, but he nevertheless did not limit himself to a patriotic appeal; he actually engaged in a detailed disputation to illustrate the advantages which would result from a free economy.

With the increasing industrialization of England in the nineteenth century, the majority of the manufacturing and the mercantile classes realized that it would be foolhardy on their part to follow the tactics which they had employed in the preceding century. They opposed that minority of their own party which continued to lobby for subsidies, bounties, and monopolies; but they centered their attack upon the country gentlemen whose corn bounty was costing them such a pretty penny. The situation was paradoxical, for they had themselves taught the landowners how to use the government to advantage. True, this instruction had been given several decades ago; but the sins of the fathers are often visited upon the children. The manufacturers maintained that the tariff upon the import, and the bounty upon the export, of corn resulted in raising the price of corn, the price of bread, and hence the price of labor. As could have been expected, the plaintiffs called Adam Smith as their principal witness, and his testimony was very valuable. He denied that the landed class derived any substantial benefit from the corn laws: he advocated that they be repealed. But he gave further testimony which for technical reasons was disallowed. His realism forced him to consider nationalistic tendencies; he therefore urged the adoption of all measures which might increase the security of the country. Economic principles must never block legislation for the defense of the realm. England, even before the beginning of the nineteenth century, was no longer completely self-sufficient regarding her food supply, and she became less so as time went on.[6] Hence in case of war the country might be forced to go on very short rations; in fact it might even suffer hunger. It is not certain that if Adam Smith had been permitted to testify in detail the jury might not have evaluated his earlier testimony differently.[7]

The landed and the commercial classes, although frequently at odds, did nevertheless work in harmony on certain issues. They were especially friendly during the period of the French Revolution when they feared that the poor might rise up against the rich, not only on the Continent but also in England. The leaders in the community therefore immediately combined to forestall any such eventuality. Just prior to the close of the eighteenth century the tyrannical anti-combination acts were passed. The common law had long prohibited combinations but the courts had used their discretion in enforcing this statute: employers were never prosecuted. Adam Smith objected to the attempts of laborers to improve their condition through concerted action, but he likewise disapproved of masters who acted in silent agreement. His sense of fair play made him resent the existence of different laws for the poor and for the rich. Hence he must have turned in his grave when he was used, or rather misused, in the anti-labor agitation of the late nineties.[8]

At about this time the spirit of the *Wealth of Nations* was again violated, for it was quoted to justify the inclosure movement which was proceeding with great rapidity. The later economists chided Smith for his naïve adherence to the physiocratic doctrine which proclaimed that nature worked along with man and facilitated his efforts when and only when he engaged in agriculture.[9] Not only did the "acute and sagacious" Smith presume that the tiller of the soil was more productive than other laborers, but he also concluded that the farming population was generally superior to city dwellers. His interest in the land led him to attack all impediments in the path of its progress and to favor all measures which led to its improvement. Smith was greatly impressed with the benefits which man derived from the division of labor, particularly because specialization was such an important timesaving device. Now, simultaneously with the industrialization of the country, a revolution on a much smaller scale took place in agriculture. The common fields were being rapidly inclosed.[10] It was assumed that if land were redistributed the cottager would lose the habits of indolence which he had acquired by sauntering after his cattle on the commons. The quarter, half, and whole days which had been imperceptibly lost in the past would no longer be wasted.[11] Smith admitted that inclosed land had the advantage of affording the cattle better pasturage and reducing the owner's cost of upkeep;[12] but it is extremely doubtful whether he would have approved of the ruthless policy of inclosures had he been aware of their cost. At the close of the eighteenth century Arthur Young, that keen observer of English agriculture, pointed out that thousands of poor people wanted to know what had happened to the house and the cow which they once possessed.[13] Smith would never have desired to add to the burdens of the impoverished.

At the best, the problem would have been difficult, for the productivity of the land could not have been substantially increased so long as parcels remained uninclosed. Perhaps upon reviewing the evidence one will conclude that the movement toward large-scale agriculture was inevitable; surely it was economically advantageous. The social incidence of the disappearance of the commons was, however, very serious; the poor were injured by nineteen inclosure bills in twenty; in some grievously injured.[14] Now the cottager was doubtless an inefficient farmer, but despite his lack of skill he was able to eke out a living for himself and his family. His tenancy gave him an established position in the institutional setting, a matter of great moment to all human beings. This status was completely undermined when his land and cottage rights were canceled. His spirit as well as his bones were destroyed.

Adam Smith was always interested in economic expediency, but he never failed to include social and ethical values in his balance sheet. Often the allocation of overhead costs turn a profit into a loss. If Adam Smith had had the opportunity to audit the inclosure movement, there is little doubt that he would have found it to be bankrupt, though perhaps involuntarily so.

Many declassed agricultural laborers found their way into the cities where they frequently obtained employment in the new factories. The mechanization of industry gave a most pronounced stimulation to general business activity and created thereby a great

demand for labor; but although the expansion continued for many years, the employment market did not
remain favorable. Women and children were able to
perform the necessary work not only as well as but
frequently better than men, for nimbleness and deft-
ness were more important than strength. Wages would
have been depressed by these new sources of supply;
the farm movement only aggravated the situation. The
cottagers who had lost their rights, and the agricultural laborers who had always been horribly underpaid, doubtless were enticed by the prospects of factory employment. During the lifetime of Adam Smith
the mobility of labor had been greatly restrained because of the Settlement Acts, and he therefore, in
line with his general labor program, had suggested
that they be modified, or even better, abolished. He
felt assured that the workers would be greatly benefited by being permitted to search for employment
wherever they desired; in the past they had all too
frequently been forced to starve at home. This restrictive legislation, however, continued in effect until
the landowners suddenly discovered that they would
gain rather than lose by its repeal; the new factories
could absorb a large number of the indigent poor, who
until now had been supported by charity. The statute
was not formally repealed; it was permitted to rest in
peace. Adam Smith's arguments were totally irrelevant. He had advocated a change in policy on the
ground that it would improve the conditions of the
working population; the law was flouted because it
proved profitable to the property owners.

The critics of modern capitalism have always painted in deep colors the dire effects of the introduction of machinery upon the laboring class of England;[15] and even the defenders of the system have seldom denied the misery and misfortune which it caused. The latter maintained that, when one considers the momentous implications of the industrialization of England's economy, a period of chaos was inevitable. No revolution has ever been completely bloodless. The socialists have always been prone to emphasize the hellish condition of this period. From time to time, authorities resent this interpretation. They suggest that wars, taxes, and famines were primarily responsible for the unhappiness of the poor.[16] But few deny that the rapidity of technological improvements in many industries embittered the life of the working people.

During the nineteenth century the leaders of British society were so anxious to excuse and to justify the events of their day that one must doubt whether their hands were absolutely clean. They showed an extreme avidity for each and every doctrine which could exculpate the new industrialism. The *Wealth of Nations* offered a veritable mine for this purpose.

Adam Smith opposed the apprenticeship statutes on the ground that they hurt both the general public and the laboring class; the price of commodities was artificially enhanced and the opportunity to establish oneself in trade was strictly limited. He therefore advocated their immediate repeal. The widespread introduction of mechanical appliances frequently depressed the price of labor. The divorce of the laborer from the

land made it very difficult for him to withstand the
attacks upon his standard of living, for refusal to accept the proffered terms of employment did not mean
privation; it meant starvation. Food, housing, fuel
could be obtained only by the expenditure of money.[17]
It is not surprising, therefore, that the calico printers
petitioned Parliament in 1804 for a stricter regulation
of their trade; they charged that the masters had been
able to reduce their wages by inordinately increasing
the number of apprentices while stringently limiting
the number of journeymen. The legislative committee
discovered after investigation that the employers had
entered upon this policy by about 1790 at a time when
no undue pressure of work existed; the masters could
only have been interested in seizing an opportunity of
lowering the wages of their workmen. The recom-
mendations of the committee were very indefinite; in
fact alternative proposals were advanced: either the
state should undertake a very strict regulation, or else
the trade should be entirely free. The members were
reluctant to press the first suggestion because they
realized that the general trend was away from governmental interference; on the other hand they were unable to close their eyes to the appalling conditions.
They were, however, convinced that the situation had
taken a turn for the worse because the apprenticeship
regulations had been permitted to lapse.[18]

A few years thereafter, the watchmakers and rib-
bon makers submitted equally doleful complaints.
They maintained that the disregard for the old
statutes had a most deleterious effect upon their welfare and the legislature upon investigation admitted

the justice of their complaint.[19] Although the government on certain occasions indicated that it might interfere on behalf of the working class, nothing materialized; the pressure from the master manufacturers was too great. The employers were constantly petitioning Parliament to repeal formally the apprenticeship statutes; and finally in 1814 after a prolonged debate the major part of the Elizabethan act was removed from the books.[20] Many who voted to scrap the statute were probably convinced that the weighty opinion of Adam Smith supported their action, for even a superficial survey of the *Wealth of Nations* could leave no doubt of the author's position on this issue. The obvious is frequently overlooked; 1776 was not 1815. It was one thing to advocate the abolition of the apprenticeship regulations at a period when they insured monopolistic privileges to a small group; it was an entirely different matter to suggest their abrogation when they formed one of the few remaining safeguards against the complete pauperization of a large portion of the laboring population. In the light of Adam Smith's prejudices in favor of the workers, it becomes doubtful whether his sentences were properly appreciated by the legislators. In 1776 laborers were generally poor; in 1815 they were frequently destitute. The legislature in repealing the Apprenticeship Acts followed the letter but not the spirit of the *Wealth of Nations*.

The importance of labor in the productive process has varied throughout the ages, but even in the most mechanized society it has retained a very great significance. In the domestic economy of Adam Smith's world, wages formed perhaps the most important element in the total cost of production; in the industrial society of the early nineteenth century they retained, despite the new machines, great significance.

During the early period of England's development, the justices of the peace had had the power to establish the remuneration for labor, and it was not until the seventeenth and the eighteenth centuries that this custom fell into disregard. Adam Smith knew of only a few isolated examples in his society where the state attempted to fix wage rates; he was in fact very happy that this usage was no longer enforced, because he felt that it had a tendency to lower wages.[21] The law had never been repealed, but it had been permitted to lapse. In 1813 the cotton weavers begged Parliament not to abolish the juridical establishment of wages, for it alone stood between them and starvation. Although the law had long been relegated to the legislative graveyard, the weavers prayed that it might be resurrected. The miracle did not come to pass and they were forced to rely entirely upon the goodness of their employers' hearts.[22]

The Scottish economist believed that the state regulation of wages had been a bane to the working class; but a few years after his death the laborers were anxious to throw themselves on the mercy of the state, for they instinctively realized that master manufacturers in Parliament would act with more consideration in their public than in their private capacities. Once again history played tricks on Adam Smith.

After Smith's death business became very unsettled, and although much of the blame could be placed upon the process of industrialization, other factors were not unimportant. The prevalence of war was a most disturbing influence. It resulted in frequent booms and depressions against which even the most cautious entrepreneur could not protect himself.

The mechanization of industry, however, was sufficient in itself to upset radically the economy of Great Britain. In the past, prices had been largely determined by the cost of materials and labor; and these had not had the habit of varying greatly within short spans of time. The situation changed as soon as capitalists invested increasing sums in machinery. Depreciation costs assumed great significance. Because of the rapidity of technological improvements, obsolescence could not be estimated with any degree of certainty; the safest but most difficult bookkeeping procedure would have been to consider plant equipment, irrespective of its cost, to be worth one pound. The pace was exhilarating but nerve-racking: rich today, poor tomorrow; more often poor today, rich tomorrow. The master manufacturers realized that the country would benefit greatly if their risks were reduced, and they therefore offered the laborers the opportunity of becoming public benefactors.

In earlier decades the working population did not live a life of luxury and contentment, for child labor, low wages, and long hours were quite usual. But about the time of the French Revolution the condition of many English laborers took a turn for the worse. And yet, during the first three-quarters of the eighteenth century, the standard of living of the workers had been rising. The introduction of machinery reversed this trend. The oversupply of hands and the complete disintegration of their monopolistic privileges were not the only factors which facilitated their impoverishment. Inflation of the currency, bad harvests, and a rapidly increasing population contributed their share to the burdens of the unfortunate.

The affliction of the laboring poor was due in large part to the fear which the new machinery engendered in the captains of industry; for, being acquainted with the history of King Midas, they distrusted their own good fortune. Power offered them the opportunity of transforming a poor country into an inconceivably rich one; but unless they were very careful they might be destroyed in the process. Business as it continued to expand became an increasingly dangerous gamble; the number and the size of the prizes had been increased, but the chances of suffering substantial losses had also been multiplied.

In preceding decades an entrepreneur had been able to go along at a fairly even pace; traditional behavior was more of an asset than a liability; but as the rapid mechanization of industry took place, one could no longer continue at the old accustomed stride. Either one kept with the vanguard or retired from the race. Man's ignorance of the machine added to the tension and the strain.

In Adam Smith's time an employer was probably personally acquainted with all of his workmen, most of his customers, and many of his fellow employers. The success of his business depended in large part upon his relations with people; it was only slightly influenced by his contact with the machine. The Industrial Revolution brought with it many and radical changes; among others a reversal in the importance of human beings and machinery. When a man was forced to invest thousands of pounds in mechanical apparatus there is little wonder that his sleep was disturbed by dreams of fixed costs. True, the machine speeded the trip to heaven; but it also reduced the traveling time to hell; unfortunately upon departing one never knew at which destination he would arrive.

The erratic behavior of business had the most unfortunate consequences for labor; for the employers, in their anxiety to insure themselves against the worst risks, forced their employees to pay the high premiums. The exploitation which took place was not motivated by the desire of the captains of industry to earn a few additional pounds; it was dictated by a belief that all profits depended upon securing the maximum productivity of labor. During the early years of the factory system the quaint wail was often heard that the entrepreneur would be ruined if his laborers passed too many hours in sleep. The expensive machine might never pay for itself even if employed twenty-four hours a day; it would surely prove a loss if it were not used at least fifteen hours.[23]

Interest rates, the price of raw products, and the demand for finished goods were one and all beyond the control of the individual manufacturer; the variable labor costs were within his control. Had the industrialist been able to restrain the fluctuations of any of the former elements, his feeling of insecurity would have been relieved. Since he lacked this power, the confused

leader decided to protect himself with the bodies of
the torpid masses.

Throughout the years when the technological
changes in industry were taking place, the harrassed
men of property seldom contemplated action which
would lead to the improvement of the laboring poor.
They would not tamper with a system which they
could not control; their fear stayed them in their
tracks. Many years passed before they recognized that
an increase in wages would not lead to their own
sudden and swift ruin; or that a shortening of the
working day would not cancel the advantages of
machinery.

The exploitation of labor did not leave the leaders
of society with a very clear conscience and it is not
surprising that they attempted to compensate for their
sense of shame. They granted the worker the sacred
right of free bargaining. If one laborer were willing
to work for ten shillings a week while another would
accept six shillings, it would assuredly be improper to
refuse the lower offer. The humanitarian principle of
the minimum wage is most inhuman because it violates the right of man to work at a rate which satisfies
both himself and his employer. The astute political
thinkers of the nineteenth century completely overlooked the fact that a head of a family could not meet
the competition of a bachelor worker. Adam Smith
had been willing to restrain his laissez faire philosophy, but his descendants refused to proceed moderately.

The family in the new industrial system disintegrated as a production but not as a consumption unit:
father, mother, and children no longer worked to-

gether; but the shillings of the father, the pence of the mother, and the farthings of the children were pooled. Time and again evidence was presented to parliamentary committees that had it not been for the paltry contributions of women and children to the running of the household, many families would have been wiped out.[24]

The economists of modern capitalism subscribed to the doctrine that wages would ordinarily be sufficient to permit laborers to fill their bellies with bad food, to cover their backs with threadbare garments, and to indulge their children in the same luxurious manner. The population of Great Britain grew very rapidly during the years of the Industrial Revolution, and one is somewhat at a loss to explain this occurrence in view of the subsistence wages which frequently prevailed. Part of the increase could doubtless be ascribed to the rising prosperity of the middle class but, despite its unusual abilities, that class could hardly have been responsible for doubling England's population during the fifty years between 1780 and 1830. Clearly this rise could never have taken place without the aid of the laboring poor. One is confronted with the interesting paradox of how it was possible for the workers to multiply if their wages were barely sufficient to keep them from starvation.

In the domestic system not a few impediments blocked the way of a rapid increase in the nation's population. It was most difficult to set up in trade without substantial capital, and it was also no simple matter to earn one's bread by the sweat of one's brow.[25] The factory system did facilitate marriages.

Many of the indigent poor obtained work, and the wives and children of the underpaid laborers were likewise able to earn a few shillings. Hence if people would work from their sixth to their sixtieth year, it was possible for them to obey the biblical injunction—increase and multiply. Numbers deal with quantities, not qualities; the census reports therefore are not as paradoxical as they at first appear. Moreover the increasing control of disease reduced the fatalities from periodic scourges.

Despite the pronounced abhorrence of the early nineteenth century for state interference with the economic organism, occasions did arise when even such worthy principles had to be thrown to the winds. Just before the end of the eighteenth century, years of agricultural scarcity came to pass, and the magistrates of the land were much perturbed by the extreme plight of the laboring poor. A meeting at Speenhamland was called for the purpose of discussing whether the justices of the peace should again exercise their powers of establishing the wages of labor. After much discussion a negative decision was reached. But some remedial action had to be taken. An allowance system was therefore created which provided that a worker must receive a specified amount of money; if he were unable to earn it by his labor, the parish would have to make up the difference.[26] To arrive at this minimum figure the size of his family and the price of provisions were to be taken into consideration.

The conference likewise suggested that all employers raise wages and, as might have been expected, the request was politely ignored. The Speenhamland system was rather quickly adopted throughout the greater part of England; the working population unfortunately was not benefited but hurt by this well-intentioned project. Employers no longer had to pay their laborers a living wage, for the community had now obligated itself to prevent their hands from starving to death. The theory of a minimum subsistence received official sanction.

The system led to the most unusual results. It became dangerous for the working population to practice thrift because aid could be obtained only if one were a pauper. Furthermore, an artisan with a little property could not receive employment from the community until he had expended every cent of his savings.[27] Shrewd landowners in an attempt to escape the burdensome poor rates frequently depopulated entire villages by demolishing cottages;[28] they imported laborers from near-by settlements to perform the necessary work in their district. The socially minded magistrates and clergymen unwittingly helped to undermine British chastity by establishing the Speenhamland system. Bastard children became very valuable; parish allowances were regulated by the numbers in a family. To marry the mother of several bastards would put a man on easy street for the rest of his life. It is not surprising that one observer remarked that the number of unmarried mothers had greatly increased.[29]

The adoption of allowances was probably introduced to alleviate the condition of the laboring class and the instigators of the project probably had not foreseen that it could have deleterious effects. Doubt-

less the workers were becoming unruly, and the reformers believed that meeting them part way might
save trouble in the end; but their actions were not
determined by considerations of expediency.

Throughout these years of storm and stress, the
laboring poor were the victims of an old but now
regenerated institution—the truck system. Adam
Smith had pointed out in the *Wealth of Nations* the
cupidity of forcing workers to accept part of their
wages in goods rather than in money. The commodities in the companies' stores were always above the
prevailing market prices in direct proportion to
the degree of the owners' unscrupulousness. The self-
appointed disciples of Smith in their ingenious attempt
to justify the system took refuge behind his general
doctrine of non-interference with the labor contract.
They suffered an interesting lapse of memory concerning his specific utterances on this subject. The British
public generally was uninitiated in the mysteries of
this exploitation; the miners in the isolated regions in
the west did not even have the satisfaction of knowing
that some old ladies sympathized with their trials and
tribulations. The most patriotic of all Englishmen,
Benjamin Disraeli, would not have exaggerated incidents which reflected unfavorably on Britannia; yet he
relates that cowed miners when they finally revolted
against the truck system were satisfied only after they
had burnt the store to the ground and spilled the
blood of the owner.[30] No one but the devil could have
led Englishmen to commit arson and murder; in fact it
seemed as if the entire cohorts of hell were arrayed
against the nineteenth-century laborers.

Smith's opinions on the state regulation of wages, the apprenticeship acts, poor relief and the like could perhaps have been twisted to justify the innovations in British government and industry which occurred after his demise. His analysis of the truck system did not offer the possibility of a double construction; yet the leaders of English society in the nineteenth century performed the impossible. They transformed labor's best friend into labor's worst enemy. Money respects no one—not even the dead.

Adam Smith became the godfather of nineteenth-century urban industrialism, although he was clearly prejudiced in favor of eighteenth-century rural civilization. Smith probably subscribed in large part to the physiocratic doctrines because they dealt sympathetically with the farming class. He much preferred the beauty of the country to the conveniences of the city; moreover he had much greater admiration for the tiller of the land than for the teller in the cage.

There is no reason to idealize the past. The farming population which Smith esteemed did not live very satisfactorily: food was not plentiful; clothing was inadequate; social intercourse difficult; labor long and arduous. But despite the comparative poverty of agricultural communities in the eighteenth century, they never approached the degradation of nineteenth-century industrial settlements.

The exploitation of men, women and children during the early years of the factory system could never have taken place in an agricultural community. Time was not unimportant to the farmer but he was in no position to convert his spare minutes into pence. He was always at the mercy of the elements and, although he might have worked with great intensity during the harvesting season, he was able to recuperate during the winter months. For even if he combined manufacturing with agricultural work, he was never under the same exacting pressure as the city slave; his long hours equaled or at least approached those of his fellow sufferer in the towns, but he was not constantly supervised and directed. If he commenced work at five or six and ceased at nine or ten, he undoubtedly could not have passed a pleasant day. But he was not fined for coming a few minutes late in the morning, nor was he throughout the day kept under lock and key. He sold his labor power; the factory hand sold his soul.

Location values are always greatest in congested communities and therefore the commercialization of space led to much greater evils in the cities than in the country. Although a farmer's cottage might not have been commodious, certainly twenty people did not sleep in one room.[31] Primitive living conditions, moreover, are much less disagreeable in the country than in the city.

The machine paved the way eventually for the general improvement in the community's standard of living; but during the first years of its reign it had the opposite result. Perhaps the momentous turmoil which accompanied the industrialization of British life could not have been avoided; but during that chaotic period the state might have attempted to exercise some control. The statesmen who refused to advocate governmental action on behalf of the poor had assuredly no right to support their position by quoting Adam Smith.

One of the most distinguished followers of the Glasgow professor impeded the passage of the most conservative labor legislation in the House of Lords by paying lip service to the general doctrines of his master.[32]

Social reformers have for obvious reasons always been interested in children. Adam Smith devoted considerable attention to child labor and education. Children in the domestic system did not lead a very happy life, for the insufficient income of their parents made it impossible for them to enjoy many pleasant things. They probably were forced to help their parents in whatever pursuits the latter happened to be engaged; but it is unlikely that they were unduly exploited. Now the Industrial Revolution brought about the greatest vicissitudes in the life of the young. Factory production created a great demand for child labor, and for the first time in history the flesh and blood of the young could be directly exchanged for pence and farthings. The extension of the money economy made it mandatory for most parents to exploit their children. The laborers could no longer grow potatoes; they could only purchase them— most frequently purchase them with the earnings of their young.

The state did not interfere but rather encouraged the employment of minors. A community could best reduce its tax rates by placing a large number of its charges at the disposal of a manufacturer. The guardians of the poor, moreover, did not exercise great care, for the children who were bound out to employers showed an appalling mortality.[33] At times, the murder of parish apprentices proved profitable because the community paid ten pounds for each child taken off its hands. One mistress, after she had worked, starved, beaten, dashed, and trampled a child to death, could obtain another without any difficulty and receive ten pounds for her trouble.[34]

Poor relief was in a most chaotic condition during the Industrial Revolution; taxes had risen substantially. As could be expected, the authorities were most anxious to reduce the rates and hence refused assistance to anyone who did not capitalize his children's earning power.[35] The state therefore abetted rather than impeded child labor. The major exploitation of children was not directly the result of governmental action; it was more closely related to the industrial structure. The wages of male laborers were so depressed that even the supplementary contributions of the women could not prevent a household from starving. The English poor therefore had to live on the earnings of their children; else they might follow the pleasant and helpful suggestion of Malthus, and practice marital restraint. The legislature could perhaps have eased if not solved many of the problems, but it saw fit to refrain from action, for ''the interests and instincts of class were disguised under the gold dust of Adam Smith's philosophy.''[36]

One of the best insights into British society during the period of the Industrial Revolution can be obtained from a study of public education. Adam Smith had been able to boast that in his day illiteracy had almost disappeared in his native country; only a very few could not read and many were being instructed in writing and arithmetic.[37] In England the common people were less well educated because there existed insufficient funds and a shortage of parish schools.

With the industrialization of the national economy, a new impediment arose in the path of popular education. Almost all children of the poor were employed and it therefore became difficult to find time to send them to school. After a working day of twelve or fourteen hours a youngster was good for nothing but his bed.

A survey of the industrial centers in the middle thirties revealed that between 10 and 20 percent of the mill hands were unable to read, and approximately 50 percent were unable to write.[38] Karl Marx, quoting from a much later report, offers some interesting evidence of the level of culture among the laboring poor in the richest country in the world. A twelve-year-old defines a king as "him that has all the money and gold." A fifteen-year-old boy who was in the habit of going to church, remembered only one name that the priest mentioned—somebody called Jesus Christ; however, he did not know anything about that person. One child remarked, "The devil is a good person. I don't know where he lived. Christ was a wicked man." A ten-year-old girl spells God, d-o-g; furthermore she does not know the name of the queen.[39]

Smith thought that an educated public was a boon to the state and that the dissemination of knowledge was the strongest bulwark against the spread of fanatical beliefs. He believed that a human being could not live a decent life unless he was able to read and to write. The leaders of British civilization during the

early years of the nineteenth century, with certain
notable exceptions, disagreed radically with Smith's
position; they favored an illiterate populace.[40] At
least they feared that widespread education might
have unfortunate repercussions. It was much safer to
leave well enough alone.

This study of labor clearly illustrates the divergence in both thought and action between the leaders
of nineteenth-century industrialism and the reformer
of eighteenth-century mercantilism. The lack of harmony is not limited to this one problem; it is a fundamental dissonance. The nineteenth century feared
action; Adam Smith feared words.

Hell called heaven.

A Dangerous Oracle

Fairy tales have their place not only in literature but also in history. The account of creation in the opening chapter of Genesis, or the recital of the miraculous acts of Jesus in the Gospels, is beautiful prose, in fact beautiful poetry. But the religious scribes have given both a historic tinge without doing any violence to the facts. No possible objection can be leveled against the scientific methodology of these writers of old; they intentionally dressed their fairy tales in historic costumes. They knew exactly what they did. They never thought it their duty to refrain from embellishing the materials which they analyzed. They spun phantasies to suit themselves, and offered apologies to none.[1]

There were men who wrote about the past in a different manner, for they desired to present a truthful narrative of the happenings of old. They did not serve the muse of the poets. Their religious worship was moreover more complicated than that of their esthete brothers, because their goddess was much more exacting in her demands.

Time has excellent curative effects upon the excesses of historical interpretation; it seldom requires decades to right a wrong, very seldom centuries. The dead remain dead for all eternity, but on occasion a long period must elapse before the souls of our an-

cestors can rest in peace. This is especially true when
for some foolish reason, having decided to overlook
the fact that they have left this world for good and
all, we continue to count them among the living.
Adam Smith is one of those unfortunate mortals who
has not come to rest in the Elysian fields, because
Charon has not yet been ordered to transport him.
Many a naïve individual probably believes that his
followers have dealt kindly with him. Upon investigation it becomes clear that they treated him
outrageously.[2]

Even a liberal-minded burgher will resent being
called father by a horde of brats when he well remembers that he never entered into matrimony. Nor
can his disturbed state of mind be soothed by testimonials which extol him for qualities which he never
possessed. His perplexity is still further increased
when he notices that his modest achievements, perhaps
worthy of some slight recognition, have been completely overlooked. Robin Hood plundered the rich;
but he also fed the hungry and clothed the naked. No
earthly reason exists why his pirating and robbing of
the wealthy should be commemorated and extolled
while his kindness and sympathy for the poor should
remain unsung. To have him become the favorite
totem of the lords and barons would be truly ludicrous.
Now such was the tragedy of Adam Smith, who was
praised by the descendants of his enemies, and scorned
by the descendants of his friends.

A hundred and fifty years and more have passed
since Smith first presented the world with his *Wealth
of Nations*, the book upon which his later fame was to

rest. Since its publication, much has been written about this treatise, but vital disagreements still exist. For once, time has not been an effective therapeutic agent; or has the period perhaps been too short? Hardly so. The relation of Hume, Voltaire, Rousseau, to the intellectual and political movements of their time has been well established and by now they have been catalogued in the eighteenth-century handbook. Adam Smith alone of all the prominent figures of that epoch is still a cause of dissension among critics. The *Wealth of Nations* resulted in the depersonalization of Adam Smith. The nineteenth century commentators, although they did not wilfully strip him of his human attributes, completely forgot that he had once been flesh and blood like themselves.

England suffered great pains during the birth of industrialism, and as the child grew her tribulations continued. The distracted mother believed that the *Wealth of Nations* might prove a good opiate—past experience had proved that it possessed sedative qualities. The difficult child matured but the parent did not know whether her offspring would lead a life of virtue or of vice. She therefore found great solace in the words of the eighteenth-century philosopher who prophesied a happy and prosperous future for it. A terrific struggle was waged in England after the death of Adam Smith and he had the misfortune to have his ghost drafted for the war. The cause of the strife was not unimportant; it centered on the issue of whether the country's industrial structure was a boon or a bane. The participants were so wrought up that they did not hesitate to employ every possible weapon. For instance, the mild-mannered essayist, John Ruskin, referred to Adam Smith as that "half-breed and half-witted Scotchman."[3] The intensity of Ruskin's re-action against the Glasgow professor leads one to believe that he must have held Smith personally responsible for the excrescences of industrialism. The esthete's misconception was not due to culpable ignorance, for the defenders and admirers of the factory system had beclouded the issue by constantly showering praise upon Adam Smith.

The middle of the nineteenth century found Eng-land most upset. The reform of existing social, economic, and political institutions was debated. For instance, the bill which restricted the working day of women and children to ten hours in order to protect them from the worst types of exploitation was first presented to Parliament early in the century. Its passage, because it was certain to take money out of the pockets of many people, was delayed until 1850.

The liberals and the conservatives employed what-ever arguments they possessed. For instance, Charles Dickens broke with tradition when he ceased to write about dukes and duchesses. He took occasion to sketch the poor and referred constantly to their exploitation; his descriptions of industrial England gained them many friends. The unctuous bourgeoisie tried to counteract the work of the novelist by proving that his lack of academic training made him incom-petent to appreciate the beautiful doctrines of the new bible—*The Wealth of Nations*—and therefore an un-worthy judge of all matters pertaining to political economy. The use to which Adam Smith was put by the avaricious capitalists resulted in the reformers' antagonism toward him. His true character was lost in the battle over property rights and class privileges.[4]

The struggles associated with modern industrialism did not end in the nineteenth century, for although certain issues may not longer be disputed, new ones have arisen. The twentieth century generally recognized the right of the state to limit the hours of work for women and children; it did not admit until recently that the governmental authority had jurisdiction over the hours of work for men. Protection for the female worker was acknowledged; protection for the male worker was denied.

Adam Smith is still with us; his well-deserved rest has again been postponed. The poor soul will probably haunt this earth as long as the system of capitalism survives, and perhaps even after it passes. A man, no matter how great his contemporary influence may be, seldom remains a dominant force in the economic and political world a hundred and fifty years after his demise. Napoleon distinctly changed the life of Naples, Poland, and the Rhineland, but Mussolini, Pilsudski, and Hitler need take little direct account of his actions.

The contribution of a prominent personality in the realm of ideas is likely to survive somewhat longer, although the duration of its effectiveness will largely depend upon the incidence of material change. Catholic theology and Aristotelian philosophy satisfied the eighth as well as the tenth century because stability in environment made for stability in thought. The nineteenth and twentieth centuries, however,

have witnessed the most marked upheavals; hence one
would anticipate the rapid obsolescence in the ideas of
old. The economic system of the eighteenth century
has all but disappeared and one would therefore
expect to find the economic theories and fancies of
that period only in a museum. One is therefore
startled to learn that a treatise on economics written
before the invention of steamboats, railroads, and
automobiles is still in vogue long after these mechanical improvements have become commonplace.
Of course, it was no ordinary treatise which survived.
Adam Smith had genius and style—indeed a very
rare combination. Now one of the most brilliant insights of Smith was doubtless his perception that the
British colonies on the west coast of the Atlantic
Ocean might one day become more important than
their mother country. Smith devoted considerable
attention to the struggling colonies, their problems
and their potentialities. He suggested a number of
reforms in British colonial policy which he believed
would benefit both London and New York. His
proposals were general; his studies specific. Indians,
rum, and free land were constantly in the background,
for these were characteristic of the new settlements.
Adam Smith's approach, like every approach, was
conditioned by the materials in hand.

A hundred and fifty years later the conditions no
longer exist but the approach is still very much alive.
Anachronisms are as frequent as they are dangerous.
The domestic economy of the eighteenth century has
been superseded by the industrialism of the twentieth.
The resemblance between the two is indeed very slight.

And yet, the attempt is constantly being made to study and reform the existing system with the tools which were developed to grapple with the old one. Perhaps the most outstanding example is that of President Hoover. Here is a firm believer in the immaculate conception of economic theories; but here is an economic theologian whose orthodoxy is neverthelesss not beyond reproach. Let us investigate.

In December, 1931, Mr. Hoover submitted his third annual message to Congress.[5] This country, in fact, the entire world, was in the throes of a serious depression; the message therefore dealt primarily with economic problems. As one would expect, neither the problems nor the analyses resemble those in the *Wealth of Nations;* the President could not model his remarks after the writings of an eighteenth-century academician. But a careful perusal will be rewarded by the interesting discovery that Mr. Hoover's message concludes with words which are almost bodily transferred from the *Wealth of Nations.*[6] Now Adam Smith's philosophy of laissez faire was very intimately associated with the economic and political structure of his day; his theory of freedom was directed against the prevailing system of restraint. The domestic economy of mercantilistic England had disappeared many decades before Mr. Hoover's birth. It is surprising, therefore, that this old theoretical apparatus had not yet been scrapped.

Herbert Hoover probably considers himself a lineal descendant of Adam Smith and therefore does not hesitate to employ the theories of the Scottish economist. The question of the relationship between these two men ought to be investigated for it might enlighten many who are not well versed in the science of genealogy.

Money has plagued all economies, but it has especially plagued those which are highly integrated. Industry and banking in a modern capitalistic country are elaborately intertwined. The President therefore in suggesting means of alleviating the depression devoted considerable attention to the banking problem. Governmental banking in the opinion of Mr. Hoover did much to support the wabbling economic institutions of the country. He was especially pleased by the results which were obtained by relief to agriculture. The Federal Farm Board, although it was unable to reverse the declining trend of prices, doubtless saved many a farmer from bankruptcy.[7]

Adam Smith would have been not a little shocked by the remarks of this student, who showed no knowledge whatever of his teachings. Smith was antagonistic towards large, centralized banking institutions, for he feared the power which such semi-monopolistic bodies might wield, and believed that the public would be much better served by a group of small competing houses. He was, moreover, violently opposed to any interferences with the mechanism of prices because he knew that whenever a clique was able to influence or control prices the consumer was hurt. Smith considered the exploitation of the general public for the benefit of the producers the very worst feature of the mercantilistic system. Prices would be lower, employment more widespread, and the prosperity of the country greater if market values could be established without any outside interference. A meager supply might occasionally force buyers to pay an enhanced price for their purchases, and an abundant supply might result in a loss to the sellers; but any attempt to remedy such conditions would only make bad worse. One of the basic doctrines of the *Wealth of Nations* was that of the implicit limitations of the control of business by the state. The government should collect taxes for the support of the crown, the courts, and the army; otherwise it should refrain, with very few exceptions, from any interference with the national economy. Herbert Hoover, a firm believer in the laissez faire philosophy, and the titular head of a party whose motto was "more business in government, less government in business," viewed with favor the interference of a Federal agency in private enterprise. In fact he recommended to Congress the advisability of increasing the scope of governmental action by increasing the capital of the Federal Land Banks. These institutions were aiding the farmer; hence their bonds ought to be stabilized by public monies. Smith would doubtless have been somewhat confused by the arguments of his descendant, for he considered the equating of supply and demand on the market the only proper and reliable method of stabilization. But the President was not perplexed; he found it possible to adhere to the general tenets of the theory of economic freedom though he disregarded their specific implications.

The decade of the twenties witnessed the rapid expansion of American industry; once the depression commenced, manufacturing and trade suffered almost as greatly as agriculture. Even before Mr. Hoover transmitted his annual message to Congress, the manufacturing and commercial activities of the country were radically curtailed. The financial position of corporations, partnerships, and private enterprises which had been vastly inflated during the boom period was now, after two and more years of liquidation, increasingly precarious. The President, taking cognizance of the situation, suggested to the legislature the advisability of establishing a Reconstruction Finance Corporation for the purpose of aiding industrial and mercantile undertakings. The capital of the relief corporation was to be supplied by the government and the applicants who could secure credit from no ordinary source would receive primary consideration.

Adam Smith in his day had feared the Bank of England because he felt assured that a large monopolistic institution was almost certain to be mismanaged; furthermore he was not pleased by the intimate relation between the Bank and the government. He believed that economy to be most efficient in which the state was passive rather than active. The plea of President Hoover that an emergency made extraordinary legislation imperative might possibly have obtained Smith's half-hearted support. It is distinctly doubtful whether he would have agreed to the government's subsidizing private industry. Smith was never oblivious to the fact that governmental action, no matter how well intentioned, frequently made bad worse, rather than better.

The eighteenth century probably witnessed alternating cycles of business activity, but these were in large measure the result of extraordinary circumstances such as wars, agricultural deficiencies, financial speculation, and the like.[8] But the economy of that day was in no way so sensitive as our own; it was less integrated. It is not surprising therefore that Mr. Hoover's constant reference to *confidence* sounds rather odd to a student of Adam Smith; the word is seldom mentioned in the *Wealth of Nations*, and then without any special significance. The President, however, justifies many of his reforms on the score that they will help to restore the public's confidence in the business structure.[9] Now assuredly the economies of the eighteenth and twentieth centuries must be radically different, because Adam Smith had no occasion whatever to be concerned with the state of public confidence. The divergence between the world of Adam Smith and the world of Herbert Hoover becomes even clearer as one continues to analyze the President's message.

Throughout the last thirty years, anti-trust legislation has had an important position in legal, economic and political discussions. The master manufacturers and merchant princes have been annoyed by the net in which they have been entangled for many years. Their freedom of movement and action has of course not been so much thwarted as impeded. Still, even spiders can sometimes make lions uncomfortable. The President remarks that he is not in favor of repealing the anti-trust laws, because he considers them a safeguard for healthy competition. At the same time

he recognizes that industries exploiting natural resources, especially coal, lumber and oil, have been
constantly demoralized because of their inability to
stamp out reckless competition. Mr. Hoover is therefore not at all certain that price-fixing and monopolistic control would be more deleterious to the public
interest than the continuance of the present destructive
methods of production and distribution.[10]

The trust was unknown in the eighteenth century;
the closest analogy which might be discovered is the
joint-stock company. Adam Smith's reaction to the
large business units of his time has never been pub-
licized, not even by his most ardent admirers. The
reason is not difficult to discover; he thoroughly
disliked them. He was of the opinion that they formed
a very serious handicap to the most efficient development of the national economy. Directors who controlled other people's money would not act carefully
nor intelligently. Despite Smith's attack on these
institutions, the modern corporation became so
firmly intrenched during the latter half of the nineteenth century that his most faithful disciple would
not venture at present to repeat his arguments.

Herbert Hoover has no right to borrow the concept
of healthy competition from the *Wealth of Nations* and
apply it to his analysis of trusts. Smith never studied
trusts because they did not exist in his day. Furthermore, in discussing their prototypes, the joint-stock
and regulated companies, he emphasized the fact that
under no conditions could he consider them to be
healthful.

The *Wealth of Nations* is permeated with the view that all economic analysis must be concerned with the benefit or harm which the public derives from the institutional structure. Upon the basis of this criterion Smith concluded that joint-stock companies should be scrapped because they lead to inefficiency and waste. His argument concerned itself with the psychology of man. Smith believed that it was a universal trait of human nature to be more interested in one's own than in anybody else's welfare; hence a business which is entirely directed by people who have invested perhaps little or no money in the enterprise is certain to be badly managed. Irresponsible leadership will undoubtedly seriously harm the public by destroying large amounts of capital.

Had Adam Smith been afforded the opportunity to review the problems of corporate enterprise in 1931 there is little doubt that his general approach would have been the same as in 1776: namely, a preoccupation with the public welfare. His conclusions might have differed greatly from those of his earlier analysis. The Scottish economist was not superstitious, nor was he ever held spellbound by tricks or shibboleths. General objectives were his major concern; techniques had only a secondary interest for him. Herbert Hoover however was enamored of the instrumentalities of economic organization; healthy competition became for him a revered totem.[11] The master and the disciple were of one flesh but not of one spirit.

During the nineteenth century, while American economists taught in the universities of the land the doctrine of free trade, the members of Congress were

occupied in passing one tariff act after another. There
is no reason to conclude a priori that the judgment of
the senators and representatives was not as sound as
that of the academicians. Nor need one assume that
the protectionists were all motivated by considerations of private gain; there were doubtless many who
sincerely believed that high duties were of distinct
advantage to American industry. They were oppressed
by the fear that because of the higher wages of American workingmen, the unrestrained import of foreign
wares would lead to unsalability of native products.
Sophisticated critics might mock at this fear, but they
could not completely dispel it.

President Hoover in his message repeats the general
argument that it would be dangerous for American
industry and labor to compete with foreign industry
and labor because the higher standards of living in this
country raise our costs of production. In his opinion
the only way to safeguard the superior economic
status of the United States is to protect this country
from European and Asiatic goods. The Chief Executive informs Congress that if any increase in protection
is deemed desirable, joint action by the Tariff Commis-
sion and himself will be able to cope with the situation.[12] The President has a perfect right to advocate
mercantilistic restrictions on foreign trade; but he
must then consider himself a follower of Sir James
Steuart, not of Adam Smith.

One of the principal objectives of the *Wealth of
Nations* was to convert England to free trade, for
Smith believed that the burdensome restraints which
the mercantilists had placed upon the movement of

goods seriously retarded the progress of the country. He was convinced that the commonwealth would advance much more rapidly if bounties and drawbacks, import and export duties, were removed. Smith realized that the change from a protectionist to a free trade society was no easy matter, and would be fought by intrenched interests. But he did not hesitate to force the issue because he decided that the majority could easily be won over to his side. His realism, however, made him contemplate an imperfect conversion, for he knew that under exceptional circumstances economic expediency would have to make way for political expediency. Industries which were essential for national defense must be protected; the public ought to be glad to pay a few pounds or even many pounds for enhanced security.

Smith's advocacy of free trade was based upon his belief that commerce does not impoverish but enrich a country. Furthermore his dislike of governmental restraints led him to advocate the more widespread introduction of personal freedom and liberty. Smith distrusted the state as much as he trusted the individual.

The *Wealth of Nations* does not contain a completely consistent body of doctrine; at the same time there are not many implicit or explicit contradictions. Unfortunately the same cannot be said for the message of President Hoover. Although he professes a sincere regard for laissez faire he does not hesitate to advocate measures which are at complete variance with his general philosophic position. Inconsistencies in systems of thought or action are to be expected. On the other hand it is rather disturbing to find anyone publicly proclaiming adherence to a specific body of doctrine at the same time that he is constantly violating its spirit. Mr. Hoover has a perfect right to advocate protective tariffs, but he does not strengthen his case by paying lip service to the economic philosophy of a freetrader.

Almost twenty billions of dollars were invested in the transportation system of the United States. The President devoted not a little attention in his message to the problem of the railroads, for the adverse trend in business had seriously undermined their financial stability. Insurance companies, benevolent trusts, and savings banks were all heavy investors in railway securities; hence a serious predicament would arise if the fiscal solvency of the roads were endangered. Mr. Hoover, recognizing the delicacy of the situation, suggested to Congress that it proceed to grapple with the emergency. Specifically, he recommended that the legislature facilitate in certain instances the consolidation of competing lines, and furthermore regulate their rates in the public interest.[13]

Governmental regulation of the railroad system has been so firmly established that even the most devoted pupil of Adam Smith would not suggest a reversal in policy. Perhaps a learned student of the *Wealth of Nations* could discover that the Scottish economist had implicitly approved governmental control of the transportation system; he had advocated the state ownership of the highways. But learning is often dangerous. To stretch the analogy from the ownership of throroughfares to the ownership of railroads is really unwarranted; Smith never proposed that the state should own stagecoaches or barges. If Smith's discussions in the *Wealth of Nations* are projected on our screen, we can possibly maintain that he would have favored state ownership rather than state control of the railroads. But Mr. Hoover would not be overjoyed at this discovery; in fact he would be disconcerted. Ideas can be stretched to a breaking point. A theory propounded seventy-five years before the farmer first asked what would happen to a train if a cow stood on the tracks, could hardly prove suggestive in remodeling the transportation system of the United States in the third decade of the twentieth century. But Mr. Hoover respected the wisdom of his ancestors.

The President was confronted with many other serious problems, but they were unfortunately problems upon which the *Wealth of Nations* could throw no light. In 1931, as in previous years, a very substantial portion of the Federal budget was devoted to veterans' relief. In the days of Adam Smith wars were even more frequent than at present; they were, however, much less severe. The national exchequer did compensate the wounded soldiers but the drain was not serious; a few thousand pounds annually took care of the disabled veterans. Mr. Hoover was forced to attack an entirely different problem; approximately one-third of the entire Federal income was expended upon the soldiers. Billions are not millions, nor millions, thousands.[14]

One of the most serious aspects of the depression was the large numbers of unemployed. In the prosperous years which preceded the debacle, several million people were unable to find work, but the problem first became acute in the fall of 1929. While the country was progressing, few observers were disturbed by what appeared to be purely a momentary dislocation; the unemployed laborers would soon again be absorbed. But when the President wrote his message in December, 1931, even the most optimistic individual was forced to reckon with the labor problem. The numbers of unemployed had greatly increased; furthermore the fact that their reserve funds were nearing exhaustion made their condition increasingly precarious. The President was therefore forced to consider the problem of relief. He believed that private charities and local governments could cope with the situation much more effectively than the Federal government. Washington could best aid indirectly. The speeding up of the public-works program and the establishment of the Reconstruction Finance Corporation would doubtless result in the creation of employment;[15] this was the proper sphere of action for the Federal government. If it exceeded these bounds local responsibility and initiative would be weakened and the basic principles which have guided this country from the first would be violated.[16] In the early days of the republic, poor relief, because of the economic structure of the country, was the concern of the local rather than of the state and the Federal governments. Mr. Hoover must have overlooked the fact that Alexander Hamilton, the founder of his own party, devoted the greater part of his life to strengthening the Federal government, and that Abraham Lincoln, the greatest of all Republicans, fought a bloody battle to demolish forever the sovereignty of the individual states. Since the Civil War the Federal government has constantly enlarged its powers at the expense of the states. Mr. Hoover therefore assumes poetic license when he discourses about the precious possession of local initiative; this gem was lost many decades ago. The President is clearly opposed to the dole, and he is perfectly entitled to his opinion. But once again his evidence does not support his case. The founders of the nation would not have been afraid, if state treasuries were exhausted, to feed the hungry citizens with Federal funds. And there is not the least reason to suspect that the unemployed would on patriotic grounds have refused to eat bread purchased with the monies appropriated by the Federal rather than by the state legislatures.

Men have often been without work. Several centuries ago approximately 20 percent of the laboring population of Great Britain was unable to obtain employment. The problem of poor relief vexed England for many years; reforms in administration, however, were very slow. From the reign of Queen Elizabeth when the principal of local responsibility was established, until the middle of the nineteenth century, no basic changes were made.

The twentieth century is not the eighteenth century, and today Federal is, in almost every respect, superior to state administration. Mr. Hoover's contention that Federal unemployment relief would be a violation of the American precepts of government cannot be substantiated. His analysis of administrative efficiency adds no weight to his position. Once again the theories of the past do not reinforce the prejudices of the present.

There is always a slight danger in indirectly distilling a man's philosophy of life from his public utterances; misinterpretation can easily result. Fortunately, Mr. Hoover in a speech delivered at King's Mountain has so clearly outlined his general position that this possibility does not exist.[17] The President sketches what he believes to have been the most characteristic phases in the development of the United States. In the opening paragraphs he informs us that there is no aristocracy in this country; man is not born to a position of distinction.[18] Doubtless there exists ample evidence to support the contention of the Chief Executive; yet this observation has no great pertinency. In England the eldest son of a baron enters the House of Lords upon the death of his father; in the United States millionaires and multimillionaires are appointed secretaries of the Treasury. Plus ça change, plus c'est la même chose.

The President prides himself that in this country the channels of opportunity are open to all, channels which if properly navigated will permit one to arrive at the land of eternal bliss. Mr. Hoover does not believe that his argument is vitiated by the fact that the courts have held three thousand dollars a reasonable monthly allowance for one child, while fifty dollars is customarily paid by relief agencies for the monthly support of a family of six members.[19]

The President is convinced that the government should play a minor rôle in the life of the community; its principal duty is to umpire. All participants in the race should start from the same point and they must not digress from the established rules during the course of the contest.[20] The government's task is not so simple as it at first appears, for society would have to undergo many changes before every member in the community would be able to compete without a handicap. For instance, it would be no easy matter to equalize the opportunities of the children of West Virginia miners and the children of West Virginia mine owners.

Mr. Hoover in discoursing on these subjects is probably greatly influenced by his personal experiences. His parents were not weighed down by earthly possessions and yet he managed to achieve the most coveted position in America. The state afforded him a free education, and the laws of the land did not restrain his freedom of movement. No wonder that he believes this country to have no equal on earth. The President assumes that the driving force in American civilization has always been individual initiative, but he does not approve of an unrestrained individualism. Were we to adopt, however, a non-individualistic political philosophy, similar to that which prevails in Soviet Russia, it would not be long before our civilization would come to an end.[21]

In his peroration Mr. Hoover appeals to Americans to preserve their system in its pristine purity, for if they surrender the ideas and ideals which have guided this nation from the day of its founding no one can foretell the evil which might come to pass. The people of the United States eat more food, wear more clothing and possess more automobiles than the people of any

other country in the world. Their prosperity is solely
the result of their unique philosophy and practice of
government.[22]

In the eighteenth century England was the most
prosperous nation on earth; hence she had many
admirers. They felt assured that the preëminent position of the country was due to the excellency of her
social and economic system. A hard-headed Scottish
economist, however, asked the mercantilistic theorists whether the nation had not progressed in spite of,
rather than because of, these institutions.

The author of the *Wealth of Nations* developed an
economic philosophy to meet the economic problems
of his day. He created a new ideology because the old
one had become outmoded and therefore useless.
Herbert Hoover attempted the reverse. He tried to
force the economic system into a framework which it
had long outgrown, forgetting in the process that the
mortification of the flesh does not lead to the ennoblement of the spirit. Forgetful oracles are dangerous
oracles.

Flesh and Spirit

The world is a terrifying place and man has often whistled to keep up his courage. Although in early times wild beasts, hostile neighbors, famines, and floods continually disturbed his peace of mind, his fear has not been solely a fear of external enemies. Despite all of these troubles he has often been upset by figments of his own imagination. Spirits, demons, and ghosts have played an important rôle in every culture. While he was living in the midst of danger, man's self-assurance could not have been very great; it is not surprising therefore that he attempted constantly to increase it. At a very early time he developed an optimistic philosophy which helped him to overcome his fear complexes. Natural calamities could not be prevented, but they could be interpreted; hence man decided that whatever happened, happened for the best. A plague which killed thousands was often considered a blessing in disguise, for if the gods had so desired, they could assuredly have leveled the entire community. If the will to believe exists, reasons are never difficult to manufacture.

And so it came to pass that in every tribe there arose a group which, conscious of men's desire to believe, helped them to accomplish their aim. The priests explained that which did not permit of explanation.

The priesthood maintained that it possessed an intimate knowledge of the ways of the unknown, and this contention when sustained by the populace had tremendous implications. Men slaughtered and were slaughtered because the spiritual intermediaries constantly revealed to them the wishes of the inscrutable. Not a few prophets shook this earth. Paul made it possible for the papacy to rule Europe; Mohammed, by preaching of Allah, led Arab horsemen to conquer half of Christendom.

Man's appeal to the unknown has not always resulted in martial strife; in fact he has upon occasion sought aid from the unknown in order to avoid warfare. People either approve or disapprove of the society in which they live. For the most part the wealthy and the powerful are satisfied to leave well enough alone; but upon occasion the aggressiveness of the poor forces them to act. Frequently both camps call upon the same deity to aid them in their struggles with their enemies.

Words can have an effect upon the mind as potent as that of the most powerful drug; many people have become addicts despite their attempts at resistance. A study of the history of such persons might facilitate the discovery of a therapy.

In modern times the unknown has often been referred to as the law of nature, natural law, the state of nature, and the law of God and of nature. But these are all words without any specific connotation. Many critics have shown a great degree of naïveté when they failed to realize that words could never have a purely formal independence. A code of ethics among churchwardens and among thieves is likely to be entirely different; little would be gained by talking of the ethical code.

In 1625 a Dutchman wrote a book on the laws of war and peace and in that volume he constantly referred to natural law and the law of nature.[1] Writers before him had frequently used these concepts, but he made them popular. His predecessors as well as his successors did not have a common point of view; natural law could mean any one of a hundred different things and could be used in a hundred different ways.[2] Mohammedans, Jews, and Christians all believe in the same God, but they are by no means in agreement as to His thoughts and actions. Does He send sinners to hell or does He not? Are the pious rewarded, and if so, in what manner? Those who pray to Allah believe that heaven flows with wine and is full of comely women with black eyes; the followers of Saint Paul have a different opinion concerning the hereafter.

The popes during their long domination of Europe maintained that men's rights depended upon the papal interpretation of God's will. After the Reformation this theory no longer went unchallenged; in fact a new and highly individualistic philosophy arose. Philosophers asserted that all humans possessed certain rights and privileges by virtue of being born, and these in no way depended upon any earthly authority.[3]

Luther's initial victory by no means ended the struggle against autocracy. It continued for many years. The eighteenth century witnessed an intensification of the strife. The reformers during this period made much of natural law and natural rights because they believed that they could strengthen their case by proving that their plans harmonized with nature. The Newtonian physics exerted a pronounced influence upon men of thought; the social scientists were greatly impressed by the physicists' belief that nature resembled a well balanced and integrated machine. They hoped that social phenomena could likewise be organized harmoniously.

Silent and spoken aspirations do not always agree and therefore words often confuse rather than illumine important issues. Even so keen a critic as Thorstein Veblen was confused by the verbiage of the eighteenth century. He believed that the Physiocrats and Adam Smith were both primarily concerned with developing the law of nature in economics.[4] The opening lines of the famous Physiocratic tracts seemingly substantiate Veblen's interpretation, for the question is there raised whether society cannot best be organized by the natural law or the moral order.[5]

France was on the edge of a precipice throughout the greater part of the eighteenth century and her intelligentsia were therefore very likely too preoccupied to have paid much attention to metaphysics. Men in order to give full expression to what Veblen calls their "instinct of workmanship" must have the advantages of a quiet environment. It does not seem probable that the philosophers, the statesmen, and the publicists of the eighteenth century desired to work out the implications of the mechanics of the natural order for economics. They thoroughly dis-

liked the existing society and therefore devoted their
major energies to reform. Perhaps certain of the
socially minded individuals even foresaw that their
own personal fortunes could be enhanced by introducing important changes.[6]

In England, the government did not oppress the
individual as greatly as in France, but it did molest
him rather frequently. Adam Smith deeply resented
the meddling of the state, and therefore took up his
cudgels. The *Wealth of Nations*, his chief offensive,
frequently refers to the natural order; in fact, unseen
hands, benevolent spirits, and the like are found
throughout the work. His doctrine of laissez faire
was perhaps a substitution for Newton's law of
gravitation. It is, however, doubtful whether Smith's
claim to fame can be based, as one critic has maintained, upon his application of the natural order to
economics.[7] There is no denying that he, as well as
the French economists, used this apparatus, but the
question must still be raised as to its significance.
Adam Smith understood *natural* to mean the causal
sequences which could be anticipated if disturbing
influences were absent; the Physiocrats employed the
word to illustrate ideal conditions which had once
existed and which they hoped would once again exist.

We are all forced to use the tools at our disposal
and it is not surprising that during the eighteenth
century radicals both on the Continent and in England
had frequent recourse to the natural order. This
concept was extremely common. Words have meaning
only in a specific context. The term *bad* conveys by itself nothing more definite than the term *natural order;*

but the statement that George III was a bad king
has just as specific an implication as Adam Smith's
statement that the economic system should be permitted to operate in accordance with the laws of
nature. The spirit is much more important than the
flesh but unfortunately it is only the flesh which remains visible after death. Critics, because they search
for concrete materials, are therefore often thrown off
the track by attempting to reconstruct solely on the
basis of the physical remains.

The reformers of the eighteenth century were one
and all likely to appeal to the natural order; however
they did so for different reasons. For instance, Rousseau's idealization of the primitives was undertaken
for the purpose of having a white background upon
which to sketch the black phases of contemporary
French culture. The restraints from which the subjects of Louis XVI suffered could be brought out in
clearer relief by discoursing upon the unlimited
freedom of the aborigines. The appalling conditions
in France until the actual Revolution got under way,
managed to unite the vast majority of liberals. In
England the situation was by no means so desperate,
and for this reason there existed very little harmony
among the intellectuals. The devotees of the natural
order were striking illustrations of the irregularities
of nature. The advocate for high tariffs and the advocate for free trade were enlisted under the same
banner; the leading exponent of mercantilistic economics used natural law to defend his position; the
leading exponent of laissez faire did likewise. These
writers doubtless believed that their pet theses if

proved to be in harmony with nature would be more readily accepted. The same natural process which equated demand and supply on the market, rotated the earth around the sun. The intellectuals, for the most part revolutionists, although they did number some conservatives in their ranks, felt assured that their pretension of understanding the workings of the unknown could not fail to aid them in their task. The mysterious has always had a peculiar fascination for man. It is not improbable that Adam Smith's references in the *Wealth of Nations* to the law of nature were a specific reflection of this common animus.

The differentiation between words and intentions is no easy matter especially when a study has to be undertaken upon a man long since dead. Perhaps the highly formal character of the eighteenth century disquisitions on the Natural Order could more easily be appreciated if one were to review a contemporary situation where the materials are more familiar. Though the Louis are no more, the law of nature has survived.

In 1931 Pope Pius issued an encyclical on Christian marriage and divorce.[8] Ever since the decline of the temporal power of the papacy, the Church has been primarily concerned with the family, for by controlling the sacrament of marriage it has been able to exert a most important influence upon its adherents. It is not surprising for the Pope to maintain that the family is more sacred than the state; in fact that man is born not for this earth, but for eternity.[9]

For many centuries Europeans believed that unless they received the last rites from a priest, they would never enter Paradise. The Protestant revolution, in popularizing the theory of predestination, managed to dispense with the services of the clergy. The divines no longer had the opportunity of sending a man to the warm regions below or the temperate zones above. The Mother Church lost many millions of followers because the masses in the northern countries no longer believed that priests could modify the decree of eternal damnation. The Church nevertheless withstood even this great secession. The erring children were forgotten and the priests immediately commenced to preserve intact that which was not upset by the Reformation. And they succeeded. The Bishop of Rome was castigated by Luther, but four centuries later the words of his successor are received with veneration by millions of his followers, and with respect by all educated people. Despite the preachings of Luther and of Calvin, many continued to believe that the only insurance for an eternity of bliss lay in obedience to the commands and counsels of the spiritual leaders of the Church. Her monopolistic position was probably largely responsible for her survival. The Pope was the earthly custodian of Christ's kingdom, and he and his priests were alone informed of the wishes of the Divine.

As long as men obeyed the priests in highly personal matters the Church had no reason to fear. In recent years, however, many of the faithful have disregarded the opinion of their priests. No wonder that His Holiness the Pope is concerned, for the very foundation of his control has thereby been attacked.

For centuries the Church has frowned upon any and every attempt to remodel the institution of marriage. In recent times divorce and contraceptives have become prevalent, and the Pope is therefore greatly disturbed by the false principles and utterly perverse morality which have led men either to ignore or to deny the great sanctity of Christian marriage. The brief submitted by the eminent prosecuting attorney is extremely interesting. The Pope quotes freely from Thomas Aquinas; but he could almost as well quote from Jean Jacques Rousseau. Does any kinship exist between medieval scholasticism and eighteenth century enlightenment?

The Pope first analyzes Christian marriage from a utilitarian standpoint. Possibly other students of the problem will after a careful survey disagree with the conclusions of the pontiff. Were he to employ only supernatural arguments his opponents could in no way touch his position; but he appeals in good Aristotelian fashion to both reason and nature.[10]

Men will not agree as to what is rational and what is natural. The Pope does not, and cannot reckon with a disunity in ultimates. The head of the Church therefore relies in large part upon supernatural argumentation to prove the universal validity of his approach. He points out, for instance, that the laws of matrimony were made by God, the author of nature; but although man has the right to decide whether he wishes to enter matrimony, once he does so he automatically becomes subject to the divine law.[11]

Many years ago Adam Smith spoke of the "author of nature" and of the "master architect." He appealed

to nature because he desired to facilitate the process
of institutional change; the pontiff appealed to
nature in order to stay change. The latter following the
Thomistic tradition maintains that man cannot
possibly transform institutions which are under the
influence of natural laws. The classical economists in
contradistinction to Smith were of like opinion. For
instance John Stuart Mill stated that man could no
more alter the laws of production than he could alter
the laws of gravitation.[12]

A major difference exists between the approach of
the eighteenth and the twentieth centuries to the
study of natural law; this dissonance can best be
illustrated by a review of the earlier period. The
writers of the French Enlightenment appealed to
nature and appealed to reason. They believed that the
autocratic powers of the crown were largely responsible for their country's misery. The king maintained that he ruled by divine right; the reformers in
their attempt to undermine his position naturally
attacked religious faith. Reason was employed to
combat faith.[13]

Men during the last century and a half have
placed much greater reliance upon the mind than
upon the soul. Trusting their intellectual perceptions,
they no longer hesitate to dissolve unhappy marriages,
nor to prevent the birth of unwanted children. In early
times men would have feared even to mention these
subjects; today they do not refer to them because
they are commonplaces. The Pope is horrified at this
brazenness and therefore throws the entire weight of
his authority against the trend; he is, however, in-

fluenced by it. For not unlike the eighteenth century philosophers, he maintains that man differs from all other living things by virtue of his rational nature.[14] Voltaire and Pope Pius are however not in complete agreement. The former placed his entire trust in reason; the latter desires to have reason coöperate with grace.[15] The Pope believes that matrimony will never be perfect unless the spouses utilize the supernatural powers of grace. This partnership of reason and grace solves not a few difficulties. Family life can be successful only if a wife is willing to obey her husband, for such is the teaching of grace. On the other hand, she need not comply with every request of her husband, for that is the teaching of reason.[16]

The pontiff is especially disturbed by the eugenicists who attempt to justify their program by appealing to reason. He is willing to admit that all efforts to improve the physical and mental qualities of future generations ought to be encouraged; but he vehemently denies that the state has the right to practice sterilization. The public authority dare not punish a man who has committed no crime.[17] The Pope overlooks the fact that intent to murder is punishable under all codes of law. Every virile insane man is a potential father, hence because of his ability to harm the state by begetting insane children, he is a potential criminal. But Christian doctrine establishes and right reason reaffirms that man has no right to mutilate any of his members unless it is for the good of the entire body. The amputation of an arm or a leg can be condoned only if it prevents death.

The popes have from very early times employed the instrument of reason; Aristotle left indelible marks upon Catholic theology. The partnership of the Logos and the Trinity has however, caused students many troublesome hours. The rational and the irrational can never be completely reconciled; reason and revelation are not equals. Divine inspiration determines the premises and therefore indirectly determines the conclusions of all problems.

Prophets preach what God has revealed; scribes elaborate the preachings of the prophets. During the last two thousand years prophets have become increasingly rare; hence religion has been forced to place much trust in scribes. Even the popes commence to discourse on the lessons of experience and the proofs of history. The Church, however, is always on guard against the eradication of the supernatural. It is not surprising, therefore, that Pope Pius after making constant use of human reason, points out that men have overestimated the independence of private judgment.[18] Hence he exhorts both the lettered and the unlettered to suffer themselves to be guided in all questions of faith and morals by the supreme pastor, the Roman pontiff who is himself guided by Jesus Christ.[19]

Matrimony has been assailed, and the pontiff therefore appeals to experience to prove that the family and the state will always benefit if this institution remains inviolable.[20] He believes that the indissolubility of marriage will preclude either partner from practicing deception, for every man will know that his ties can never be broken.[21] But experience might lead one to believe that the simplification of the divorce procedure would lead to a decrease rather than an increase in adultery.

Pope Pius quotes approvingly the statement in Corinthians that true love never falls away.[22] It is therefore surprising that he insists upon the in dissolubility of marriage; this emphasis would be unnecessary if one could really trust the everlasting powers of true love. The Pope is, however, anxious to have the secular authority force people to continue to share bed and board even if true love has been extinguished; the present generation must make sacrifices for the next. Once again, one can invoke, as did the Pope, the oracle of experience, but once again one can interpret her words differently. When spouses no longer respect each other, and seek companionship outside the home, their children can no longer greatly benefit by their formal marriage.

One of the early Bishops of Rome declared that marriage even in a state of nature could not be dissolved by the civil authority; his successor in the twentieth century quotes this statement approvingly.[23] But the anthropological reconstructions of the Bishops of Rome can hardly be validated. The state of nature is a concept, and, like all concepts, it will differ according to the temperament of the artists. No wonder therefore that the works of Aristotle, Aquinas, Rousseau, Smith and Pope Pius differ, in fact, differ greatly. But His Holiness Pope Pius is sorely vexed that certain emancipated spirits doubt his interpretation. He troubles to confound the skeptics.

In the first place he points out that anything
intrinsically against nature can under no circumstances become conformable with nature.[24] Now the
conjugal act is destined by nature for the begetting of
children and any frustration of this natural power is
therefore shameful and vicious. Contraceptives thwart
nature; hence the Pope is violently opposed to their
use. Any interference with the act of intercourse is an
offense against the laws of God and nature. Every
argument can be reversed. It is quite possible to accept
the Pope's premises and arrive at entirely different
conclusions. To prevent the sex impulses of man from
finding expression is assuredly a frustration of nature;
hence the Church's doctrine of continence is clearly
opposed to the law of nature.

Birth control, because it violates natural and divine
law, is condemned by the Church as something intrinsically evil; all evidence in support of this practice
is irrelevant, for intrinsic evil can never be transformed. The plea of poverty or of health cannot
justify the use of contraceptives; no possible extenua-
tions can exist. Abortions are yet more horrible, even
when medical science approves. The physician is
frequently confronted with a situation where to the
best of his knowledge the failure to perform an operation will lead to the death of both the mother and
the unborn child. The Pope quotes scripture: thou
shalt not kill; the life of each is equally sacred. Even
admitting therefore the reasonableness of the Church's
ethical code to value equally the life of the born and
the unborn, opposition to an abortion ought not to
exist. Failure to act will result in two deaths; the

physician can probably save one life. Now the Pope himself would admit that the preservation of life is one of the first laws of nature; hence his attitude toward abortion is not in accord with natural law.

In the opinion of the pontiff, the world has departed in recent years from the straight and narrow path of virtue. Sound philosophy and sacred theology prove, however, that in order to retrace its steps the world must again adhere to the divine plan which is the exemplar of the right order.[25] The interpreter of the plan is of course the Church.[26]

There is a daily increase in the corruption of morals and the degradation of the family; the true order of things has been inverted.[27] The confusion is especially great in those lands where communism reigns supreme. Unless the world quickly seeks the good life, it will witness the most colossal upheavals.

Many years ago French peasants were being choked to death by the ministers of Louis XVI. A few patriotic citizens were determined to prevent the complete annihilation of the poor and the oppressed. In order to arouse enthusiasm for their program, the radicals of the eighteenth century drew an idyllic picture of what the world had once been, and what it might once again be, if men would only free themselves from the despots. Their propaganda helped to bring about the Revolution.

Conditions in England did not parallel those in France; the poor were better fed, clothed, and housed. Hence the populace did not cry for blood. People desire the scalps of kings and ministers only when they have no other possible means of satisfying their

emotions. The laboring poor did, however, desire
Parliament to improve their condition, and at least
one writer sympathized with their objective. Adam
Smith set out in the *Wealth of Nations* to contribute
his share to this worthy cause. Now Smith was a very
shrewd man and a very keen student of human nature.
Hence he well realized that little could be gained by
whimpering and sobbing. He himself had been
brought up in a strict Presbyterian community where
self-reliance and self-help were considered the two
most important virtues.

Smith appreciated, perhaps unconsciously, that if
his efforts were not to be entirely in vain it would be
necessary for him to camouflage his appeal. The master
manufacturers and merchant princes would never give
up part of their wealth in order to improve the condition of the petty artisan and the tenant farmer. Smith
knew, however, that if the majority of the citizens
could be convinced that his proposals would enhance
their welfare his reforms might more easily be
achieved.

The Scottish economist employed all the tricks of
the trade. Paul promised the converts eternal bliss;
Smith promised them greater wealth: Paul used water
for baptism; Smith used natural law and natural
rights. Both men were, however, much more interested in their results than in their apparatus.

Adam Smith loved life, not words. The world
after him forgot what the world before him had
known:

> the letter killeth
> but the spirit giveth life.

Appendices

APPENDIX I
English Economic Life in the Eighteenth Century

In the early chapters of this work, we presented a rather schematic picture of English economic society during the lifetime of Adam Smith. Have we done violence to the facts? Yes and no. In attempting to appreciate the approach of Adam Smith it was necessary to outline *his* conception of eighteenth-century England. Now it is of course possible that the Scottish economist was not well informed about the industrial structure of his day; hence in following his analysis we could have been led astray, yea far astray.

Modern students of English economic history (compare especially E. Lipson) are becoming increasingly convinced that mercantilism was rapidly disintegrating as early as the beginning of the eighteenth century. The implications of this point of view are of great importance in evaluating the work of Adam Smith for, were they substantiated, we must conclude that Smith was an academician engaged not in surgery but in pathology. If mercantilism were on the verge of expiring, Smith's task was truly unimportant. There is little sense in operating on a person whose heartbeat is no longer audible. On the other hand, if the economic system of restraint was still alive and virile, the Scottish economist performed a very significant service. The evidence is unfortunately self-contradictory.

One cannot deny that at the time of Adam Smith's birth many mercantilistic institutions were in a state of decay; that, furthermore, during his lifetime others disintegrated. But as Held (*Zwei Bücher zur socialen Geschichte Englands*, p. 389) pointed out, English economic life after the middle of the eighteenth century was not transformed by atrophy. Held took pains to differentiate between two aspects of mercantilism; internal and external (p. 493). Now during the eighteenth century the state supervision of wages, of merchandise, and of apprentices was becoming increasingly lax. It was, however, during the latter half of this century that the Navigation Acts were amended. Furthermore, trade with France on a legitimate basis became possible only after 1786 (Lipson, *The Economic History of England*, III, 114). In 1788 penalties upon the export of sheep or wool were made more severe than they had been in the past (compare Lipson, p. 34). Throughout the century restrictions on colonial industry and trade were frequent. In 1750 Parliament, at the behest of native iron manufacturers, prohibited the erection of iron plants in the colonies (compare Lipson, p. 191). In 1732 the inhabitants of the British settlements in America were prohibited from exporting hats (compare Lipson, p. 192). During the period under review, bounties were granted with no pronounced hesitation. We could of course quote much of Lipson which would tip the scales in the opposite direction. However, this much is clear. Adam Smith was not doing violence to the facts when he centered his attention on mercantilism; the system was sufficiently alive to warrant his consideration. Like all students of natural or social phenomena he selected certain and neglected other data. For instance, he devotes many pages to a study of the large trading corporations. Now, as he himself pointed out, several of these companies were well-nigh defunct because the interlopers had succeeded in obtaining the most profitable part of their trade. At the same time, the East India Company was still a very considerable organization. Smith therefore was not dealing with the records of ancient institutions when he analyzed the various trading companies. Reformers are forced to focus their attack upon anachronistic institutions, for they are frequently more interested in eradicating that which is old and outmoded, than that which is new and fashionable.

The other side of the picture had now best be reviewed. Mercantilism was still a sufficiently vital force in the eighteenth century to warrant the attention which Adam Smith gave it. Did Smith, however, overlook a technological revolution which was proceeding under his very eyes? If he were guilty of such an oversight, there would be ample grounds to doubt the importance of his economic analysis. Lipson is the chief of the prosecuting staff (compare p. 54, footnote 6, where he takes Adam Smith to task for having failed to take account of certain inventions). Lipson points out that in the first decade of the eighteenth century, iron ore was smelted with coke instead of charcoal; he fails, however, to add that the iron trade not only failed to advance but perhaps during the first half of the century actually declined (compare Cunningham, *English Industry and Commerce*, 2d ed., II, 461; Ashton, *Iron and Steel in the Industrial Revolution*, p. 236). In the second decade Newcomen invented the steam engine to drain mines, but Smith gave no clear intimation that he knew of this discovery. His silence is, however, not difficult to appreciate when one remembers that Newcomen's invention was of no immediate importance; it was not until Watt perfected the separate condenser that the machine became significant. Lipson informs us that the fly shuttle and spinning by rollers were invented during the fourth decade. These improvements were likewise of no immediate consequence. Lipson himself remarks (p. 249, footnote 1) that Paul's spinning and carding machines did not come into general use. We are therefore forced to conclude that Smith's oversights were not very serious. In fact we are forced to evidence our skepticism of Lipson's general contention that there is no hiatus in economic development. There is no hiatus in any development. We are all directly related to Adam and Eve. Now it is doubtless true that "the inventions of the late eighteenth century were the outcome of a long series of industrial experiments" (Lipson, p. 53). But it is not clear how paying respect "to the efforts of the earlier pioneers" will help us to appreciate the incidence of rapid technological changes upon the general economic structure.

APPENDIX II

The Effect of Machinery on the Laboring Poor

Certain writers have denied that an Industrial Revolution occurred in England toward the end of the eighteenth century. We have, however, in Chapters VIII and IX accepted the older theory which recognized such an event. Evidence in support of this latter point of view may be obtained from a study of the condition of the laboring population during the period when the technological changes were supposedly very rapid. The literary historians, with very few exceptions, have long assumed that the rapid introduction of machinery had at first a most deleterious effect upon the standard of living of many workers. Engels, Marx, Toynbee, Held, the Webbs, the Hammonds and a host of other writers have been convinced that the majority of English laborers suffered grievously from the technological improvements which took place. In 1898-99 Bowley published in the *Journal of the Royal Statistical Society* a study of the wages of English agricultural laborers. His figures included the larger part of the period which we describe as the Industrial Revolution. At about the same time, G. H. Wood published in the *Economic Journal* a corresponding study of the wages of industrial laborers. N. J. Silberling, in the *Review of Economic Statistics*, October Supplement, 1923, reworked the figures of Bowley and Wood and added many others of importance. Using 1790 as a base of 100, Silberling charted the rise of commodity prices during the following years. In 1813 his index is above 200 (Chart I). When Bowley's and Wood's figures are readjusted to this base they fail to show an equally rapid rise. But Silberling has more pertinent data. He has developed a cost-of-living index to which the indices of industrial and agricultural wages could more properly be compared (compare p. 236 footnote 2; p. 250):

Year	Cost of Living	Industrial Wages	Agricultural Wages
1790	100	100	100
1795	130	114	127
1800	170	129	156
1805	154	144	188
1810	176	170	198
1816	135	160	190

These statistics do substantiate the contention of the literary historians that the condition of the laboring groups became worse during the last years of the eighteenth and the early years of the nineteenth centuries. But we know that this period not only witnessed important technological changes, but also a very prolonged war and very insufficient harvests. These two latter factors could easily explain the lowering of the real wages of labor. In no case do the figures prove that a very marked deterioration in the standards of living of the working population took place. We assumed, nevertheless, in Chapter IX, that during these years many British laborers were in a most distressed situation. Composite figures are frequently confusing. Sections of the laboring population doubtless benefited by the rapid stimulation which their trades received from the use of machinery. But there can be no doubt that when handicraftsmen had to compete with the power machine, conditions became unspeakably bad (compare Held, p. 448). Unemployment figures must also be considered in attempting to arrive at the standard of living of the laboring poor. During the early years of the nineteenth century one-third of the weavers in Manchester were without steady employment (compare Held, p. 456).

Much additional evidence could be introduced on both sides. The conclusion which Clapham reached in his study of the trend of *agricultural* wages between 1794 and 1824 might perhaps be accepted, with one important modification, for the general trend in wages during this period: "there were important areas in which it [the potential standard of comfort] was definitely worse, others in which it was probably worse, and many in which the change either way was imperceptible" (compare *The Economic History of Modern Britain* p. 131). The one important modification is this: the numbers of laborers, especially *industrial* laborers, whose real wages had fallen during this period were perhaps larger than Clapham assumed.

APPENDIX III

Natural Law: Adam Smith and Pope Pius XI

The relation of an author's technique to an author's objective is not easily determined. But if criticism desires to do more than evaluate the logical arguments which are spread across the printed page, it must venture to guess at this relation, even at the cost of frequently, perhaps usually, guessing incorrectly.

How significant was the use of natural law in the *Wealth of Nations?* What rôle did it play? There can be no doubt that Smith became indoctrinated rather early in life with the Hutcheson brand of natural-law philosophy; in the course of his studies he probably sampled other varieties. Hence, when he commenced to cast his economic analysis into form it was almost inevitable that he use the framework which he knew best. It should not surprise us, therefore, that the rationalistic Scottish economist introduced benevolent spirits into his treatise, nor should we be startled to discover that many of his discussions center around the natural course of specific economic activities. At the risk of being tedious we must, however, point out that the tools with which a man works, although they doubtless set specific limitations upon the nature of his construction, nevertheless in no way determine the construction. Adam Smith did not desire to produce a work of art. He was first and foremost a moralist. In the struggle between Adam Smith and natural law both participants were injured; Smith received a few superficial scratches; natural law received some very deep wounds.

Adam Smith seldom permitted himself to be carried away by the potency of philosophic concepts; he remained master of the situation. Pope Pius XI in his famous encyclical (compare Chapter XI) is another striking example of man's ability to keep afloat in the sea of words.

Natural law has long had a very significant place in Catholic theology, but natural law, despite its venerable age, has not yet emancipated itself from positive law. According to one learned authority, natural law is "that which can be known by reason without the assistance of revelation" (compare *Dictionnaire de Théologie Catholique*, tome Géme, p. 879). But if perchance reason arrives at two conclusions which are mutually exclusive then it must receive aid from revelation (compare *Dictionnaire*, p. 878).

The issue is clearly posed in the question which was submitted to Saint Augustine: has a woman the right to commit adultery (at the behest of her husband) in order to save his life?

Natural law maintains that life ought to be saved; on the other hand positive law maintains that adultery ought not to be committed. Now clearly the relative importance of these ultimates can only be determined by the help of grace. The Pope, as the spiritual head of Catholic Christendom, has high regard for natural law; but he has still higher regard for positive law. Logic must bow to grace.

Notes

1. *Life of Adam Smith*, by John Rae, London, 1895, is still the most exhaustive biography. The material which has come to light since Rae's time has not necessitated any basic revision of his analysis. It was a son of Voltaire's friend who came to study with Smith in 1761. Cf. p. 59.

2. In the *Wealth of Nations* (edited by Edwin Cannan, 5th ed., London, 1931) Smith analyses in some detail the English universities of the eighteenth century. Doubtless his description is in good part the result of his reflections upon his own collegiate experiences. Cf. II, 249 *et seq.*

3. Cf. Rae, *op. cit.*, p. 144.

4. *Ibid.*, p. 179.

5. *Ibid.*, p. 253.

6. There is some reason to believe that this opinion was shared by Smith himself. *Ibid.*, p. 436.

7. As Goethe wrote in Faust:
   > "Mein Freund, die Zeiten der Vergangenheit
   > Sind uns ein Buch mit sieben Siegeln
   > Was ihr den Geist der Zeiten heisst
   > Das ist im Grund der Herren eigner Geist
   > In dem die Zeiten sich bespiegeln."

8. Marx's own approach made it impossible for him to outline the socialistic state. According to his economic interpretation of history—government, culture, and art are all reflections of the existing means of production. Hence, no one can foresee the nature of a socialistic state until socialistic means of production have become established.

9. In the fascinating *Letters of Hernando Cortez* (The Argonaut Series, New York, 1929) the intrepid Spanish explorer points out that he would have been unable to subjugate the Mexians, if God had not so willed. He emphasizes how greatly his army was outnumbered by the forces of the natives. He for-

gets, however, that European cannon were probably as important in his conquest of the barbarians as the will of
God. Cf. pp. 14, 43.

10. *Adam Smith, 1776-1926*, The University of Chicago Press, 1928.

CHAPTER I

1. *Wealth of Nations*, I, 457.

2. *Ibid.*, p. 386.

3. *Ibid.*, p. 458.

4. *Ibid.*, p. 391.

5. *Ibid.*, p. 457.

6. *Ibid.*, p. 97.

7. *Ibid.*, p. 408.

8. *Ibid.*, II., 147.

9. The Seligman Library of Economics contains scores of
pamphlets on the woolen trade, the majority of which were
published during these ten years. Doubtless, conditions had
suddenly become serious.

10. *The Danger of Great Britain and Ireland Becoming Provinces of
France*, London, 1745-6, passim.

11. Rae, *op. cit.*, p. 2.

12. *Wealth of Nations*, I, 418.

13. *Ibid.*, p. 424.

14. *Ibid.*, II., 143

15. *Ibid.*

16. *Ibid.*, Vol. I, pp. 422-23.

17. *Ibid.*, p. 419.

18. *Ibid.*, p. 421.

19. *Ibid.*, p. 400.

20. *Ibid.*, p. 341.

21. *Ibid.*, pp. 427 *et seq.*

22. *Ibid.*, p. 433.

23. *The Natural Interest of Great Britain, Part II, The Second Edition*,
London, 1748, pp. 55-56.

24. *Ibid.*, Dedication.

25. *Political Discourses*, David Hume, 2d ed., Edinburgh, 1752,
p. 68.

26. *The Political and Commercial Works*, Charles D'Avenant, London, 1771, I, 31.

27. *Account of Application to Parliament on Neglect of their Trade by Merchants of London*, London, 1742, passim.

28. *The Complete English Tradesman*, 4th ed., II, 138.

29. *Wealth of Nations*, I, 438.

30. *Ibid.*

31. *Ibid.*, p. 437.

32. *The Universal Merchant*, London, 1753, establishes as a universal social maxim, "That the Wealth of a Nation is the common Benefit of its Neighbors, and that where Commerce flourishes, the People neither merit Envy, nor are to be feared"; cf. Dedication.

33. *Wealth of Nations*, I, 458 *et seq.*

34. *Ibid.*, p. 64.

35. *Ibid.*, II, 160.

36. Rae, *op. cit.*, p. 350 *et seq.*

37. *Wealth of Nations*, I, 389 *et seq.*

38. *A Concern for Trade*, John Newball, Stamford in Lincolnshire, 1746 (?), p. 6.

39. *A Political Essay upon Commerce*, David Bindon, Dublin, 1738, p. 39.

40. *Laws and Policy of England Relating to Trade*, George Whately (?), London, 1765, p. 9.

41. *The Natural Interest of Great Britain*, *op. cit.*, p. 46.

42. *The National Merchant*, John Bennett (?), London, 1736, p. 2.

43. *Linnen Manufacture*, Patrick Lindesay (?), London, 1735, passim.

44. *An Impartial Enquiry into Woollen Manufactories*, 4th ed., Lincoln, 1744, J. Gee, passim.

45. *Reasons for Restraining Use of Gold and Silver Lace*, London, 1743, passim.

46. David Bindon, *op. cit.*, p. ix.

47. *Report of the Council of Trade in France*, London, 1744, p. 20.

48. *Discontents Occasioned by Convention with Spain*, London, 1739, p. 3.

49. Rae, *op. cit.*, p. 73.

50. *Wealth of Nations*, II, 24.
51. *A Letter to Dion* (Mandeville), London, 1732, p. 33.

CHAPTER II

1. *Manifest der Kommunistischen Partei*, p. 109 in *Lohnarbeit u. Kapital* Zweite auflage, Reclam, Leipzig.
2. Rae, *op. cit.*, p. 8.
3. *Ibid.*, pp. 417-18.
4. *Wealth of Nations*, I, 20.
5. *Ibid.*, p. 129.
6. This remark illustrates that Smith was not too greatly impressed with the advantages of a minute division of labor.
7. *Wealth of Nations*, I, 357.
8. *Ibid.*, II, 167.
9. Rae, *op. cit.*, p. 119.
10. *Ibid.*, p. 115.
11. *Wealth of Nations*, I, 51.
12. *Ibid.*, p. 146.
13. *Ibid.*, p. 362.
14. *Ibid.*, pp. 360-61.
15. *Ibid.*, II., 161 *et seq.*
16. *Ibid.*, p. 173.
17. *Ibid.*, I, 362-63.
18. Cf. Veblen's *Theory of the Leisure Class*, passim.
19. *Wealth of Nations*, I, 368.
20. *Ibid.*, p. 320.
21. *Ibid.*, II, 16.
22. *Ibid.*, I, 426.
23. *Ibid.*, II, 18.
24. *Ibid.*, I, 392.
25. *Gentleman's Magazine of 1742*. Quoted in Furniss, *Position of the Laborer in a System of Nationalism*, pp. 188-89.
26. *Wealth of Nations*, I, 193 *et seq.*; also Bindon, *op. cit.*, p. 13.
27. *Wealth of Nations*, II, 43.
28. *A General History of Trade* (Defoe), London, 1713, pp. 15-16.
29. *A Letter to a Member of Parliament, relating to a Bill for Opening of Trade from Persia through Russia*, London, 1741, p. 3.

30. *Wool and Woolen Trade Reviewed*, London, 1743, title page.
31. *The Golden Fleece*, 4th. ed., London, 1739, p. 13.
32. *Ibid.*, p. 14.
33. *Considerations upon the State of our Affairs* (Lord Littleton), London, 1739, p. 3.
34. *An Appeal to Caesar on the Nature of Public Affairs*, London, 1746, p. 23.
35. *A Letter to Lord Commissioners of Trade and Plantations*, London, 1747, pp. 8-9.
36. *The Important Question, Enquiry into the True Interest of England*, London, 1746, p. 13.
37. *Reflections on Naturalization*, Josiah Tucker, Part II, p. 26.
38. *An Essay or Method to Pay the National Debts*, London, 1744, p. 2.
39. *Memoirs of Wool*, John Smith, London, 1747, I, iii.
40. *The Landlord's Companion*, William Allen, London, 1742, *passim.*
41. *Ibid.*, pp. 7-8.
42. *Wealth of Nations*, I, 359.
43. Allen, *op. cit.*, p. 16.
44. *Ibid.*, 42.
45. *The Axe Laid to the Root of the Tree*, London, 1743, p. 6.
46. *The Case between the Clothiers, Weavers, and other Manufacturers*, Philalethes, London, 1739, p. 38.
47. *The British Merchant* (Charles King), 2d ed., London, 1743, p. 168.
48. *Ibid.*, p. 179.
49. *Wealth of Nations*, I, 393.
50. *Lectures of Adam Smith*, ed. by Cannan, Oxford, 1896, p. 169.

CHAPTER III

1. *Wealth of Nations*, II, 92.
2. *Ibid.*, I, 1.
3. *Ibid.*, p. 9.
4. *Ibid.*, p. 35.
5. *Ibid.*, pp. 52-53.

6. Cf. V. G. Simkhovitch, *Marxism vs. Socialism*, Chap. XII, for an analysis of the Marxian theory of value.

7. *Wealth of Nations*, I, 2.

8. Furniss, *op. cit.*, p. 8.

9. *Wealth of Nations*, I, 122 *et seq.*

10. *The London Tradesman*, R. Campell, London, 1747, pp. 301 *et seq.*

11. *Ibid.*, p. 22.

12. *Ibid.*, pp. 331-40.

13. *Ibid.*, p. 313.

14. *Ibid.*, p. 337.

15. *Wealth of Nations*, I, 123.

16. *Ibid.*, p. 124.

17. *Ibid.*, p. 131.

18. *Ibid.*, p. 64.

19. *Ibid.*, II, 22.

20. *The History of the Poor*, Richard Burn, London, 1764, Chap. III.

21. *Ibid.*, p. 55.

22. *England in Johnson's Day*, M. Dorothy George, New York, 1928, p. 113.

23. *Ibid.*, p. 112.

24. *To Pay Old Debts without New Taxes*, London, 1723, pp.14-15.

25. Burns, *op. cit.*, p. 136.

26. *To Pay Old Debts*, *op. cit.*, p. xxix.

27. Furniss, *op. cit.*, p. 98.

28. *View of Frauds, Abuses and Impositions of Parish Officers*, London, 1744, passim.

29. *An Account of Several Workhouses*, 2d ed., London, 1732, sheds much light upon this development.

30. *An Enquiry into the increase of Robbers*, Henry Fielding, London, 1751, *passim.*

31. *A Scheme for the better Relief and Employment of the Poor*, London, 1765, p. 24.

32. *Wealth of Nations*, I, 142.

33. Burns, *op. cit.*, p. 8.

34. *Wealth of Nations*, I, 132.

35. *Ibid.*, p. 143.

36. The Supreme Court of the United States was more than one hundred years behind the times when at the end of the nineteenth century, the constitutionality of similar legislation was reviewed. It was more Smithian than Adam Smith himself.
37. *Wealth of Nations*, I, 68 *et seq.*
38. *Ibid.*, p. 144.
39. *Ibid.*, II, 365.
40. George, *op. cit.*, p. 110.
41. Philalethes, *op. cit.*, p. 20.
42. *Bill for General Naturalization*, London, 1748, Appendix.
43. *Lectures on the Industrial Revolution in England*, Arnold Toynbee, London, 1884, p. 68.
44. *Wealth of Nations*, I, 80.
45. Furniss, *op. cit.*, p. 135; the reference is to Arthur Young.
46. *Wealth of Nations*, II, 10.
47. *Ibid.*, p. 346.
48. *Ibid.*, p. 10.
49. *Ibid.*, p. 67.
50. *Ibid.*, I, 100.
51. *Six Centuries of Work and Wages*, J. E. T. Rogers, London, 1901, p. 488. Rogers is one of the few economic historians who maintain that during the seventeenth and eighteenth centuries the fortunes of the laboring class were being constantly reduced. The contemporary evidence denies the validity of Rogers' contention.
52. *Wealth of Nations*, I, 80.
53. Rogers, *op. cit.*, p. 489.
54. *Wealth of Nations*, I, 83.
55. *Ibid.* Cf. also *The London Tradesman*, *passim.*
56. *Wealth of Nations*, II, 143.
57. *Ibid.*, p. 423.
58. *An Account of Several Workhouses*, *op. cit.*, p. 185.

CHAPTER IV

1. The significance of money in the workings of an economy is made clear if the events of this depression are reviewed. For

instance on March 4, 1933 the banking crisis imperilled the entire commercial and industrial processes of the country.

2. Cf. (*Die protestantische Ethik und der Geist des Kapitalismus*, pp. 17-206) in *Gesammelte Aufsaetze zur Religionssoziologie*, Max Weber, Tuebingen, 1922.

3. *Wealth of Nations*, I, 390.

4. Karl Marx in the *Communist Manifesto* compliments the bourgeousie on its achievements during this period.

5. *Wealth of Nations*, I, 414.

6. Cf. Cortez, *op. cit.*, *passim*, for a contemporary description of these robberies by one of the principal brigands.

7. Smith refers to the famous, better infamous, Navigation Acts. Cf. *Wealth of Nations*, II, 78. For his general analysis of the colonial question, cf. Book IV, Chap. VII, Parts I, II.

8. *Wealth of Nations*, II, 93.

9. *Ibid.*, Book IV, Chap. VII, Part III.

10. *Ibid.*, p. 433.

11. Davenant, *op. cit.*, II, 10 *et seq*.

12. *Wealth of Nations*, II, 135.

13. *Ibid.*, I, 75.

14. *Ibid.*, II, 137 *et seq*.

15. *Ibid.*, p. 233.

16. *Ibid.*, Book V., Chap. I, Part III, Art. I. For the best modern discussion of these trading companies, see *The Economic History of England*, E. Lipson, London, 1931, Vol. II, Chap. II.

17. *Considerations upon the East-India Trade*, London, 1701, *passim;* also *The Absolute Necessity of Laying Open the Trade to the East Indies*, London, 1767, *passim*.

18. *Considerations upon the East-India Trade*, *op. cit.*, p. 25.

19. *Wealth of Nations*, II, 242.

20. *Ibid*, pp. 244-45.

21. *An Account of the Subscriptions to the South Sea Company*, 1722, *passim*.

22. *Ibid.*, p. 3.

23. *Wealth of Nations*, II, 241.

Chapter V

1. Cf. Lipson, *op. cit.*, II, 371.
2. *The Draper Confuted*, London, 1740, p. 7.
3. *Ribnick vs. McBride*, 48 Sup. Ct. 545; Justice Stone's dissenting opinion is very much a rewording of Smith's position.
4. *Wealth of Nations*, Book I, Chaps. I, IV.
5. *Ibid.*, I, 63.
6. *Ibid.*, p. 129.
7. *Considerations upon the East-India Trade*, *op. cit.*, p. 5.
8. *Wealth of Nations*, II, 46-47.
9. *Ibid.*, I, 136.
10. Toynbee, *op. cit.*, p. 70.
11. *Wealth of Nations*, I, 148-49.
12. *Lectures of Adam Smith*, *op. cit.*, p. 130.
13. *Wealth of Nations*, I, 459.
14. *Ibid.*, p. 312; *Lectures*, *op. cit.*, p. 195.
15. *Wealth of Nations*, II, 16 *et seq.*
16. *Ibid.*, I, 71.
17. *Ibid.*, pp. 249-50. This discussion forms the peroration of Book One; its position increases its significance.
18. Rae, *op. cit.*, pp. 350 *et seq.*
19. *Wealth of Nations*, II, 159-60. These passages must also be weighted very heavily because they form the conclusion of Smith's attack on mercantilism. They are found for the first time in the third edition (1784), although they were published in the preceding year in pamphlet form together with three or four other "very considerable additions." Cf. Rae, *op. cit.*, p. 362.
20. *Argument upon the Woolen Manufacture of Great Britain*, Dublin, 1737, p. 3.
21. *A Brief Essay on Trade*, Josiah Tucker, 3d. ed., London, 1753, p. 74.
22. *Wealth of Nations*, II, 172.
23. *Ibid.*, I, 84.
24. *Ibid.*, pp. 248-49.
25. *Ibid.*, II, 39.

Chapter VI

1. Ecclesiastes, I: 18.
2. *Religion and the Rise of Capitalism*, R. H. Tawney, New York, 1926, *passim*.
3. George, *op. cit.* pp. 55 *et seq.*
4. Furniss, *op. cit.*, *passim*.
5. George, *op. cit.*, p. 57.
6. *Wealth of Nations*, I, 17.
7. The eighteenth century liberals were uncritical of the limits which circumscribed the perfectability of man.
8. *Wealth of Nations*, I, 249.
9. *Ibid.*, p. 83.
10. *Lectures of Adam Smith*, *op. cit.* pp. 255 *et seq.*
11. *Wealth of Nations*, II, 267.
12. *Lectures*, *op. cit.*, pp. 256-57.
13. *Wealth of Nations*, II, 273. Smith probably did not over-emphasize the importance of public opinion. He might have advanced the argument in order to secure advantages for the laboring poor which would have been difficult to obtain without first neutralizing the fears of conservative citizens.
14. *Ibid.*, p. 267.
15. *An Inquiry into the Melancholy Circumstances of Great Britain*, London, 174 [?], p. 42.
16. *Ibid.*, p. 144.
17. *Wealth of Nations*, II, 270.
18. Rogers, *op. cit.*, based his analysis of work and wages upon the records of the land owned by Oxford University, many of which were very old.
19. *Wealth of Nations*, II, 250.
20. *Ibid.*, p. 251.
21. George, *op. cit.*, p. 41.
22. *Wealth of Nations*, II, 260.
23. *Ibid.*, p. 266.
24. Rae, *op. cit.*, p. 23.
25. George, *op. cit.*, p. 40.
26. Rae, *op. cit.*, p. 21.

27. *The Querist*, George Berkley, London, 1750, p. 21. Abraham Flexner in his recent volume on *Universities*, Oxford, 1930, p. 285, points out that competition did raise the standards of the colleges.

28. *Wealth of Nations*, p. 260. Adam Smith while professor at Glasgow received an annual salary of seventy pounds and his fees amounted to an additional hundred pounds. Cf. Rae, *op. cit.*, pp. 48-49.

29. *Ibid.*, p. 261. Despite this severe criticism of foreign travel it must not be forgotten that Adam Smith spent two years abroad as tutor to the Duke of Buccleugh for which he was most liberally remunerated. Cf. Rae, *op. cit.*, pp. 164 *et seq.*

30. *Ibid.*, p. 288.

31. Max Weber, *op. cit.*, *passim.*

32. Tawney, *op. cit.*, p. 84.

33. *Short Specimen of a New Political Arithmetic*, London, 1734, p. 16.

34. *Villany Unmasked*, London, 1752, p. 37.

35. *Ibid.* Fielding talks of the priests seducing the common people's allegiance to the state.

36. *Wealth of Nations*, II, 288.

37. *Ibid.*, p. 274.

38. Rae, *op. cit.*, pp. 54, 133.

39. *The Letters of David Hume*, ed. by Greig, Oxford, 1932, II, 450 *et seq.*

40. Rae, *op. cit.*, pp. 311 *et seq.*

41. *Ibid.*, p. 307.

42. *Ibid.*, pp. 342-43.

43. *Wealth of Nations*, II, 278.

44. Cf. George, *op. cit.*, pp. 33 *et seq.*, for a description of Wesley's power over the people.

45. While Smith was teaching at Glasgow, a great civic agitation developed in connection with the establishment of a theater. The university faculty was drawn into the discussion. It is interesting to learn that Smith sided with the conservatives despite the fact that later in life he favored the presentation of drama for the public. Smith probably did not change his

views on this subject during the intervening years. At Glasgow, he felt that deference must be paid to public opinion and therefore opposed the establishment of the theater.

The intellectual radicals of the eighteenth century were careful not to offend (willfully) the prevailing prejudices. Francis Hutcheson, Adam Smith's teacher, in writing to Hume admonished the Edinburgh philosopher to be more prudent. The latter replied that he desired to keep on good terms with even the strictest and most rigid. Cf. Greig, *op. cit.*, pp. 34, 37. Daniel Defoe explained in the introduction to *Moll Flanders* that he related many incidents which might shock the public, only to illustrate the dangers of evil. Actually, he had to pay his respects to the prevailing moral prejudices before he dared tell of Moll Flanders' private life.

46. *Wealth of Nations*, II, 281 *et seq.*
47. *Ibid.*, p. 297.

CHAPTER VII

1. Helvetius was forced by the censor to reduce the number of his quotations from Hume. Cf. Greig, *op. cit.*, p. 304.
2. Rae, *op. cit.*, pp. 189, 190.
3. *Ibid.*, p. 208.
4. *Ibid.*, p. 372.
5. Greig, *op. cit.*, pp. 410-11.
6. *Ibid.*, p. 246.
7. *Ibid.*, p. 409. Baron d'Holbac was responsible for having the book translated.
8. *The Theory of Moral Sentiments*, Adam Smith, Bohn Standard Library, London, 1880, with biographical memoir of the author by Dugald Stewart. Cf. p. xvi.
9. *Lectures of Adam Smith*, *op. cit.* p. 171.
10. *Ibid.*, p. 169.
11. Rae, *op. cit.*, p. 212. "Vous verrez un philosophe moral et pratique; gai, riant à cent lieues de la pédanterie des nôtres."
12. *The Theory of Moral Sentiments*, *op. cit.* p. xvii.
13. Rae, *op. cit.*, p. 45.
14. Greig, *op. cit.*, pp. 470, 526.

15. *The Theory of Moral Sentiments, passim.*
16. *Wealth of Nations*, I, 77.
17. *Ibid.*, pp. 109 *et seq.*
18. *Ibid.*, II, 64-65.
19. *Ibid.*, I, 285.
20. *Ibid.*, p. 328.
21. *Ibid.*, II, 32.
22. *Ibid.*, Book II, Chap. III.
23. *Ibid.*, II, 184.
24. *Proposals to Preserve the Public Roads*, Phil Anglus, London, 1750. Cf. Title Page: "A brief Discourse shewing that Inland Trade is the chief Support of Societies, consequently the Support of the Nation."
25. *Wealth of Nations*, II, 217.
26. *Ibid.*, I., 338.
27. *Ibid.*, II, 203.
28. *Ibid.*, I, 395.
29. *Adam Smith, 1776-1926, op. cit.*, p. 65.
30. Rae, *op. cit.*, p. 147.
31. *Lectures, op. cit.*, p. . 205.
32. *Reflections upon the Present Unhappy Circumstances of Ireland* (John Browne), Dublin, 1731, *passim;* also *Some Considerations upon Trade*, London, 1715, p. 3.
33. *An Essay upon the Improvement of the Woollen Manufacture*, London, 1741, p. 7.
34. *Considerations on the War*, London, 1742, p. 50.
35. *Man a Machine*, De La Mettrie, translated from the French, 2d ed., London, 1750, *passim.*
36. *Lectures, op. cit.*, p. 83.
37. *A Scheme to Prevent the Exportation of Wool Unmanufactured*, Henry Laybourne, Stamford (1742), *passim.*
38. *De juri belli et pacis*, Grotius, 1625. Bonar (*Philosophy and Political Economy*, London, 3d ed., reprinted, 1927) groups together as natural-law philosophers such different people as Machiavelli, More, Bodin, Grotius, Hobbes, Harrington, Locke, Hume and Adam Smith. Obviously the term becomes meaningless if one follows this procedure.

39. Professor Wesley Clair Mitchell of Columbia University, in his lecture course on "Current Types of Economic Theory," presents this point of view.
40. Adam Ferguson. Cf. Rae, *op. cit.*, p. 138.
41. *Ibid.*, pp. 273-80.

Chapter VIII

1. *English Industry and Commerce*, W. Cunningham, Cambridge, II, 260.
2. Rae (*op. cit.*, p. 87) remarks that Glasgow was a provincial town of 23,000 inhabitants.
3. *Ibid.*, p. 89.
4. *Wealth of Nations*, I, 271.
5. *Ibid.*, p. 262.
6. *Ibid.*, p. 119.
7. *Ibid.*, p. 243.
8. *Ibid.*
9. *Ibid.*, p. 168.
10. *Ibid.*, II, 358.
11. *Ibid.*
12. *Ibid.*, I, 166 *et seq.*
13. Rae, *op. cit.*, p. 285.
14. Buckle checked the *Parliamentary History of Great Britain* in order to discover the references to either Adam Smith or the *Wealth of Nations*. He found a large number. However, a study of these passages proves that Smith's basic philosophy was not even appreciated by his admirers. The overwhelming number of direct and indirect quotations pertain to technical proposals which Smith advanced in Book V of the *Wealth of Nations*.
15. Rae, *op. cit.*, p. 289.
16. *Ibid.*
17. One member of Parliament pointed out that if the poor were to rise the honorable gentleman would prefer the riot act to the *Wealth of Nations*. Cf. *Parliamentary History*, XXXIII, 825.
18. The doctrines which helped precipitate the French Revolution were traced to Tucker, Adam Smith, and Stewart. Cf. *ibid.*, XXX, 330.

19. Cunningham, *op. cit.*, II, 452.
20. Lipson, *op. cit.*, III, 114.
21. Cf. Appendix I.
22. Smith added them to the third edition of the *Wealth of Nations*. These additions were also published separately in order that the owners of the earlier editions might purchase them cheaply. Seventy-eight of these eighty pages dealt with mercantilistic problems; if mercantilism had been dead Smith would never have devoted so much space to the problem.
23. Malthus devotes a considerable portion of Chapter XVI of his first edition to a criticism of Adam Smith, or as he prefers to call him, Dr. Adam Smith.
24. *Principles of Political Economy and Taxation*, David Ricardo, Everyman's Library, p. viii.
25. *Principles of Political Economy*, from the 5th London ed., New York, 1870, pp. 5, 6.
26. *Das Kapital*, Hamburg, 1922, p. 88, footnote 80.
27. Ricardo, *op. cit.*, p. 1.
28. Marx, who admired Ricardo, had no use for Say.
29. *The Tables Turned*, James Bonar, London, 1926, *passim*.
30. *Wealth of Nations*, p. 432.
31. *La Formation du radicalism philosophique*, Halévy, E., Paris 1901, *passim*.
32. *Essay on Population*, Malthus, Everyman's Library, Books I & II.
33. *Zwei Bücher zur socialen Geschichte Englands*, Adolf Held, Leipsig, 1881, p. 142.
34. Ricardo, *op. cit.*, p. 41.
35. *The Place of Science in Modern Civilization*, Thorstein Veblen, New York, 1930, p. 61.
36. "Approaches to History," *Political Science Quarterly*, V. G. Simkhovitch, Dec., 1929, and subsequent issues.
37. Mill, *op. cit.*, p. 537.
38. *Ibid*, p. 40.

Chapter IX

1. Toynbee, *op. cit.*, *passim*.
2. *Instinct of Workmanship*, Thorstein Veblen, New York, 1922, Chap. V.
3. Cunningham, *op. cit.*, II, 346.
4. *Ibid.*, p. 384.
5. *Industry and Trade*, Alfred Marshall, Lodon, 1919, Appendix D.
6. *Cambridge Modern History*, New York, 1907, Vol. 10, p. 760.
7. Lipson (*op. cit.*, II, 455) refers to this phase of Smith's analysis. He fails, however, to point out that it was after the writing of the *Wealth of Nations* that England became very dependent upon grain imports. This factor makes Smith's general thesis of protection for defense exceptionally important.
8. *English Economic History Select Documents*, ed. by Bland, Brown and Tawney, London 1914, p. 634. It was not until 1824 that the Anti-Combination Act was repealed.
9. *Principles of Political Economy*, J. R. McCulloch, Edinburgh 1849, 4th ed., p. 175. The commentator calls this discussion perhaps the most objectionable in the entire *Wealth of Nations*.
10. Cunningham, *op. cit.*, II, 371.
11. *Select Documents*, *op. cit.*, p. 533.
12. *Wealth of Nations*, I, 151.
13. *Select Documents*, *op. cit.*, p. 537.
14. *Ibid.*
15. *Das Kapital*, *op. cit.*, *passim*.
16. *The Perspective of the Industrial Revolution*, E. Lipson, p. 10.
17. *An Economic History of Modern Britain*, J. H. Clapham, Cambridge, 1926, p. 118.
18. *Select Documents*, *op. cit.*, p. 573 *et seq.*
19. *Ibid.*, pp. 588 *et seq.*
20. *Ibid.*, pp. 577 *et seq.*
21. *Wealth of Nations*, I, 132.
22. *Select Documents*, *op. cit.* p. 576.
23. *Marxism vs. Socialism*, V. G. Simkhovitch, New York, 1923, pp. 123-24.

24. *The White Slaves of England, Compiled from Official Documents*, John C. Cobden, 1853, p. 143.
25. Lipson, *op. cit.*, III, 436.
26. *The Village Labourer*, J. L. and Barbara Hammond, London, 1911, pp. 161 *et. seq.*
27. *Ibid.*, pp. 225 *et seq.*
28. Clapham, *op. cit.*, p. 100.
29. *The Village Labourer, op. cit.*, pp. 228-29.
30. *Sybil, passim.*
31. Cobden, *op. cit.*, pp. 416 *et seq.*
32. Earl of Lauderdale. Cf. *The Town Labourer*, J. L. and Barbara Hammond, London, 1917, p. 166.
33. Lipson, *op. cit.*, III, 434; Cobden, *op. cit.*, Chaps. III-IV.
34. Cobden, *op. cit.*, p. 204.
35. *The Village Labourer, op. cit.*, p. 150.
36. *Ibid.*, p. 142.
37. *Wealth of Nations*, II, 220.
38. *The Town Labourer*, p. 54, footnote 3.
39. *Das Kapital, op. cit.*, p. 221.
40. *The Town Labourer*, pp. 56-59.

Chapter X

1. Cf. Preface to *Old Wives' Tale*, Arnold Bennett.
2. The essay of J. M. Clark, "Adam Smith and the Currents of History" in *Adam Smith, 1776-1926*, is, in the opinion of the writer, by far the best piece of Smithian interpretation. But Clark's contention that perhaps the strongest feature of the *Wealth of Nations* is its theory of value and distribution cannot be admitted.
3. Quoted by Glenn Morrow in "Adam Smith: Moralist and Philosopher," in *Adam Smith, 1776-1926*, p. 165.
4. *The Factory Controversy*, Harriet Martineau, Manchester, 1855, p. 36.
5. *New York Times*, Dec. 9, 1931, p. 21.
6. *Ibid.*, col. 8.
7. *Ibid.*, col. 2.

8. Petty refers to a seven-year cycle. Cf. *Tracts*, Dublin, 1769,
   p. 29: "and the medium of seven years, or rather of so many
   as makes up the cycle, within which dearths and plenties
   make their revolution."
9. *New York Times*, Dec. 9, 1931, col. 3.
10. *Ibid.*, col. 5.
11. *Ibid.*
12. *Ibid.*, col. 7.
13. *Ibid.*, col. 5.
14. *Ibid.*, col. 6.
15. *Ibid.*, col. 2.
16. *Ibid.*, col. 8.
17. *Ibid.*, Oct. 8, 1930, p. 16.
18. *Ibid.*, col. 1.
19. *Ibid.*, Feb. 8, 1933, p. 16, col. 2.
20. *Ibid.*, Oct. 8, 1930. p, 16, col. 3.
21. *Ibid.*
22. *Ibid.*, col. 2.

CHAPTER XI

1. Grotius, *op. cit.*, *passim*.
2. *Natural Rights*, David Ritchie, London, 1924, *passim*.
3. *The Constitution of a Perfect Commonwealth*—T. Spence 2d ed.,
   London, 1798: "Social laws therefore can never proscribe
   natural rights," p. 12.
4. *The Place of Science in Modern Civilization*, Thorstein Veblen,
   pp. 89-114.
5. *Ephemerides*, Paris 1767, I, 3.
6. "Physiocrates," Norman J. Ware, in *American Economic Review*, Dec. 1931, pp. 607-20.
7. "Laissez-Faire," Jacob Viner, in *Adam Smith*, *1776-1926*, p.
   118.
8. *New York Times*, Jan. 9, 1931, pp. 14-16.
9. *Ibid.*, p. 15, col. 1.
10. *Ibid.*, p. 14, col. 1.
11. *Ibid.*
12. Mill, *op. cit.*, p. 40.

13. "Approaches to History, II," V. G. Simkhovitch, *Political Science Quarterly*, Dec., 1930, *passim*.
14. *New York Times*, Jan. 9, 1931, p. 14, col. 2.
15. *Ibid.*, col. 6.
16. *Ibid.*, col. 3.
17. *Ibid.*, p. 15, col. 1.
18. *Ibid.*, col. 6.
19. *Ibid.*
20. *Ibid.*, p. 14, col. 5.
21. *Ibid.*
22. I Corinthians, 13:8.
23. *New York Times*, Jan. 9, 1931, p. 14, col. 4.
24. *Ibid.*, col. 7.
25. *Ibid.*, p. 15, col. 4.
26. *Ibid.*, p. 14, col. 5.
27. *Ibid.*, p. 15, col. 8.

Index of Names

Index of Names